OECD *Economic Surveys*
Electronic Books

The OECD, recognising the strategic role of electronic publishing, will be issuing the OECD *Economic Surveys*, both for the Member countries and for countries of Central and Eastern Europe covered by the Organisation's Centre for Co-operation with Economies in Transition, as electronic books with effect from the 1994/1995 series -- incorporating the text, tables and figures of the printed version. The information will appear on screen in an identical format, including the use of colour in graphs.

The electronic book, which retains the quality and readability of the printed version throughout, will enable readers to take advantage of the new tools that the ACROBAT software (included on the diskette) provides by offering the following benefits:

- ❑ User-friendly and intuitive interface
- ❑ Comprehensive index for rapid text retrieval, including a table of contents, as well as a list of numbered tables and figures
- ❑ Rapid browse and search facilities
- ❑ Zoom facility for magnifying graphics or for increasing page size for easy readability
- ❑ Cut and paste capabilities
- ❑ Printing facility
- ❑ Reduced volume for easy filing/portability

Working environment: DOS, Windows or Macintosh.

Subscription: FF 1 800   US$317   £200   DM 545

Single issue: FF 130   US$24   £14   DM 40

Complete 1994/1995 series on CD-ROM:

FF 2 000   US$365   £220   DM 600

Please send your order to OECD Electronic Editions or, preferably, to the Centre or bookshop with whom you placed your initial order for this Economic Survey.

W9-BSZ-346

OECD
ECONOMIC
SURVEYS

1994-1995

AUSTRIA

ORGANISATION FOR ECONOMIC CO-OPERATION AND DEVELOPMENT

ORGANISATION FOR ECONOMIC CO-OPERATION AND DEVELOPMENT

Pursuant to Article 1 of the Convention signed in Paris on 14th December 1960, and which came into force on 30th September 1961, the Organisation for Economic Co-operation and Development (OECD) shall promote policies designed:

- to achieve the highest sustainable economic growth and employment and a rising standard of living in Member countries, while maintaining financial stability, and thus to contribute to the development of the world economy;
- to contribute to sound economic expansion in Member as well as non-member countries in the process of economic development; and
- to contribute to the expansion of world trade on a multilateral, non-discriminatory basis in accordance with international obligations.

The original Member countries of the OECD are Austria, Belgium, Canada, Denmark, France, Germany, Greece, Iceland, Ireland, Italy, Luxembourg, the Netherlands, Norway, Portugal, Spain, Sweden, Switzerland, Turkey, the United Kingdom and the United States. The following countries became Members subsequently through accession at the dates indicated hereafter: Japan (28th April 1964), Finland (28th January 1969), Australia (7th June 1971), New Zealand (29th May 1973) and Mexico (18th May 1994). The Commission of the European Communities takes part in the work of the OECD (Article 13 of the OECD Convention).

Publié également en français.

3 2280 00481 3663

Table of contents

Introduction   1

I.   A strengthening recovery   3

The recovery in perspective   3
Uneven demand developments   3
Production   11
Early recovery in the labour market   12
Stubborn inflation   15
Deteriorating external balance   17
The short-term outlook   20

II. Macroeconomic and structural policies   24

Overview   24
Monetary and exchange rate policy   24
Fiscal policy   29
Structural reform   40

III. Mobilising labour resources   42

Avoiding ratcheting-up of unemployment   42
Making better use of potential labour resources   49
Summing up   52

IV. Challenges for the business sector   53

Introduction   53
Business sector performance   54
Meeting new competitive challenges   74
The sheltered sector and the impact of European integration   86
Summary and agenda for further reform   98

V. Conclusions   102

Notes   109

Bibliography   115

Annexes
   I.   Technical notes   118
   II.   Supporting material to Part IV   123
   III.   Industrial classifications   130
   IV.   Chronology of main economic events   133

Statistical annex and structural indicators   137

Boxes

1.   The new fiscal programme   39
2.   The Chamber system   47
3.   Challenges for the tourism sector   61
4.   Integration effects of EEA participation and EU membership   87

Tables

Text

  1.   Demand and output   6
  2.   Household income, saving and consumption   10
  3.   Output by sector   11
  4.   Labour supply and demand   14
  5.   Wages and prices   15
  6.   Current account of the balance of payments   18
  7.   Capital account of the balance of payments   19
  8.   Economic projections to 1996   21
  9.   The Federal budget   30
 10.   Net lending of the general government   31
 11.   The budgetary impact of EU accession, 1995   34
 12.   Non-employment rates for different population segments, 1991   50
 13.   International comparisons of business sector structure   54
 14.   The structure of the Austrian business sector   57

15. Trade in manufactures and market services 60
16. Factor intensities in manufacturing production and trade 62
17. Business sector productivity 66
18. Innovative activity 68
19. Distribution of industrial enterprises and employment
    by enterprises size 70
20. Firm size and performance 71
21. Government aid to the business sector 73
22. Entry and exit rates of firms 77
23. The commodity composition of trade with Eastern Europe 82
24. Direct investment flows by region 83
25. Education and earnings in Austria and Central-Eastern Europe 84
26. Distribution margins in Austria and Germany 94
27. The macroeconomic effects of EU entry 97
28. The effect of the internal market on the services sector, 2000 98

Annexes

A1. Structural characteristics of market services 124
A2. Largest industrial enterprises of Austria 125
A3. Capitalisation of companies listed on the Vienna Stock Exchange
    by industry 126
A4. Regional structure of Austrian foreign trade from 1920 to 1992 127
A5. Telecommunications in selected countries 128
A6. Trade margins, costs and earnings by enterprise size 128
A7. Import structure and tariff regime 129

Statistical annex and structural indicators

A.   Gross domestic product 138
B.   General government income and expenditure 139
C.   Output, employment and productivity in industry 140
D.   Retail sales and prices 141
E.   Money and banking 142
F.   The Federal budget 143
G.   Balance of payments 144
H.   Merchandise trade by commodity group and area 145
I.   Labour-market indicators 146
J.   Public sector 147
K.   Production structure and performance indicators 148

Diagrams

Text

1. Current and previous recoveries compared 4
2. Exports by destination 5
3. Business sector growth and investment 7
4. The recovery in the business sector 9
5. Employment, unemployment and wages 13
6. Inflation 16
7. Saving and investment 19
8. Currency movements, interest rate spreads and inflation differentials with respect to Germany 26
9. Interest rate developments 27
10. Currency flow and short-term interest differential 28
11. Government net lending and the cyclical position 33
12. Government deficit and debt scenarios 37
13. Unemployment persistence 43
14. Unemployment benefit replacement rates net of tax, 1991 45
15. Manufacturing employment and unemployment 46
16. Relative wage developments in subsectors of industry 48
17. Early retirement and invalidity pensioners 51
18. Sectoral employment trends 55
19. Relative price levels between Austria and the OECD 58
20. Relative price levels between Austria and the EU 59
21. Export market shares of selected manufactures 63
22. Export specialisation in manufacturing 64
23. Labour productivity in Austria and Germany 67
24. Economies of scale and scope in the manufacturing sector 72
25. Relative gross direct investment 74
26. Relative importance of the equity market 76
27. University graduation 80
28. Trade with Central and East European neighbours 81
29. Policy convergence in the process of European integration 88

Annex

A1. Government revenue and the cyclical sensitivity of the budget balance 120

BASIC STATISTICS OF AUSTRIA

THE LAND

Area (1 000 sq. km)	84	Major cities, 1991 census (thousands of inhabitants):	
Agricultural area (1 000 sq. km) 1993	35	Vienna	1 540
Exploited forest area (1 000 sq. km) 1993	32	Graz	238
		Linz	203
		Salzburg	144
		Innsbruck	118

THE PEOPLE

Population 30-6-93, thousands	7 993	Net migration, 1992, thousands	37.0
Number of inhabitants per sq. km	95	Total employment,[1] monthly average 1993, thousands	3 054.9
Net natural increase, 1993	12 710	of which:	
Net natural increase per 1 000 inhabitants, 1993	1.6	in industry[2]	656.1

PRODUCTION

Gross domestic product in 1993 (Sch billion)	2 118	Industrial origin of GDP at market prices, 1993 (per cent):	
GDP per head, US$	22 784	Agriculture	2.3
Gross fixed capital formation in 1993		Industry	26.5
Per cent of GDP	24	Construction	7.6
Per head, US$	5 497	Other	63.6

THE GOVERNMENT

Per cent of GDP in 1993:		Composition of Federal Parliament (number of seats)	
Public consumption	19.2	Socialist party	65
General government current revenue	48.6	Austrian People's party	52
Federal government debt, end 1993	52.4	Freedom party	42
		Greens	13
		Liberal Forum	11
		Last general election: October 1994	

FOREIGN TRADE

Exports of goods and services		Imports of goods and services,	
as per cent of GDP, 1993	37.9	as per cent of GDP, 1993	36.8
Main exports in 1993 (per cent of merchandise exports):		Main imports in 1993 (per cent of merchandise imports)	
Food, beverages, tobacco	3.3	Food, beverage, tobacco	4.8
Raw materials and energy	5.0	Raw materials and energy	9.0
Machinery and transport equipment	39.0	Machinery and transport equipment	37.7
Chemicals	9.0	Chemicals	10.4
Other finished and semi-manufactured products	43.7	Other finished and semi-manufactured products	38.1

THE CURRENCY

Monetary unit: Schilling		Currency units per US$, average of daily figures:	
		Year 1994	11.42
		March 1995	9.90

1. Wage and salary earners.
2. Including administrative personnel.
Note: An international comparison of certain basic statistics is given in an annex table.

Introduction

The recession was rather mild in Austria and the upturn, which began in the first half of 1993, is well under way, driven both by the international recovery and growing business confidence. The established credibility of the exchange-rate link to the Deutschemark has allowed monetary conditions to ease, supporting the recovery, although as in Germany the process of interest rate reductions came to a halt in May 1994. Fiscal policy has continued to exert an expansionary influence; but with the output gap narrowing, there is now a need to correct the substantial deficit in the general government budget, which threatens the achievement of the Maastricht convergence targets. EU membership, which took effect on 1 January 1995 will have important benefits for Austria, but the budgetary costs have strengthened the need for fiscal consolidation in other areas.

Provided the fiscal situation is corrected, the economy seems set for several years of solid growth, with low unemployment and moderate inflation. This prospect nevertheless disguises important structural problems which need to be addressed if the joint challenge of EU membership and integration with eastern Europe are to be successfully met. These relate, firstly, to the labour market, where Austria shares with other European economies the tendency for unemployment to persist once it has risen, and where labour force participation is low, particularly among women and the over 50s. They relate, secondly, to excess regulation, barriers to entry and lack of competition in the service sectors, the effects of which have been to impede job creation. At the macroeconomic level, the main expression of these defects has been price inertia in the sheltered sectors, which has prevented Austria's inflation rate from falling as fast as elsewhere; at the micro level, the result tends to be a relatively low level of enterprise creation and innovation which may impede the process of adapting to greater international competition.

Part I of the *Survey* looks at recent trends and sets out the Secretariat's short-term projections. Macroeconomic policies are discussed in Part II, together with the progress recorded in areas of structural reform affecting the public sector. The problems faced in preventing a secular rise in the rate of unemployment as the economy recovers and in mobilising persons outside the labour force are analysed in Part III. The theme of the special structural subject covered in Part IV, is ''Challenges for the business sector'', which focuses on the problems faced and the reforms needed in adapting Austria's financial and human capital resources and its framework of business-sector regulation to the new international challenges. Conclusions are presented in Part V.

I. A strengthening recovery

The recovery in perspective

The recovery of output which began in the second quarter of 1993 has so far been more robust than the previous recovery – although far weaker than that of the mid-1970s (Diagram 1). The output gap has already begun to close, whereas in the previous recovery it continued to widen for some time after production had resumed growing (see further in Part II). The recovery appears to be driven more strongly than usual by capital expenditure, reflecting both the sharpness of the drop in business investment at the time of the trough and, to some extent, the subsequent unusually early pick-up. Exports have also developed dynamically – but not more than usual for an Austrian recovery.

In contrast, private and public consumption did not experience a discernible trough but continued to grow steadily if not spectacularly – much as in the previous recovery. Since employment appeared to recover slightly more quickly than normal, and the labour force to expand less than usual, the unemployment rate began falling rather early in the current recovery, though this improvement seemed to falter in the course of 1994. Thus, the current recovery displays many of the characteristics of a normal Austrian recovery led by exports, standing out principally because of the unusual strength of investment activity and the early turnaround in the labour market.

Uneven demand developments

Buoyant merchandise exports and investment activity

Rapid growth of exports reflected the pick-up of export markets. After contracting in the first half of 1993, markets for Austrian manufactured exports

3

Diagram 1. **CURRENT AND PREVIOUS RECOVERIES COMPARED**

Volume indices, trough = 100

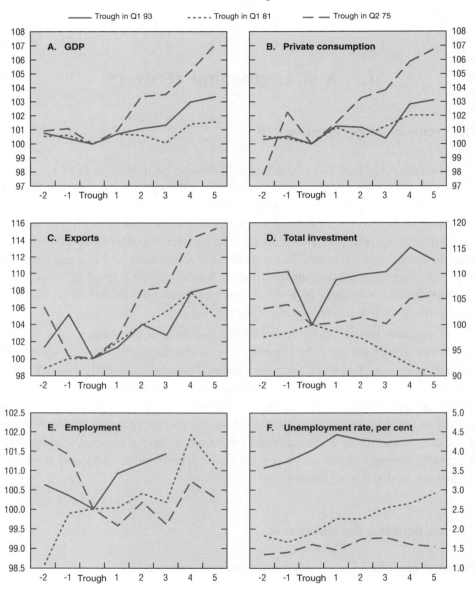

——— Trough in Q1 93   ····· Trough in Q1 81   — — Trough in Q2 75

A. GDP

B. Private consumption

C. Exports

D. Total investment

E. Employment

F. Unemployment rate, per cent

Source: OECD, *National Accounts.*

4

accelerated sharply, to grow at an average of almost 9 per cent (a.r.) in the first half of 1994 and only slightly less in the second half. There have been wide disparities in the growth of different export markets in recent years, partly because of the increased desynchronisation of business cycles, but also because of the emergence of new rapidly growing export markets. Reflecting these differences, Austrian merchandise exports to North America, Central and eastern Europe and the Far East have been considerably more buoyant than those to traditional European markets (Diagram 2). The share of Austrian exports going to these markets has increased from 14.9 per cent in 1990 to 18.6 per cent in the first half of 1994. Nevertheless, the pick-up in market growth up to the second half of 1994 largely reflected the resumption of import demand in Austria's traditional markets – predominantly Germany, which in 1993 accounted for about 40 per cent of Austria's exports of goods. Given the export- and investment-led recovery of that country, markets for investment goods and intermediate goods were particularly buoyant.

Diagram 2. **EXPORTS BY DESTINATION**[1]

Index, average 1992 = 1

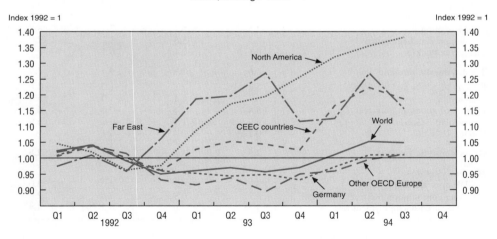

1. Seasonally adjusted, by value.
Source: OECD, *Monthly Statistics of Foreign Trade.*

With their international competitiveness, as measured by relative unit labour costs in a common currency, deteriorating slightly between the first half of 1992 and the autumn of 1994, Austrian manufacturers sustained small losses in market shares during 1993 and 1994. Total exports of goods developed broadly in line with manufacturing exports, reflecting the latter's dominant share (91 per cent), as well as strong exports of raw materials; but weakness in services exports led to a more moderate overall export volume growth of less than 4 per cent for 1994 as a whole (Table 1).

The decline in services exports in 1994 reflected problems in the tourism industry of both a cyclical and a more structural nature (salient features of the tourism industry and the problems affecting it are discussed in Part IV). The former relate both to a deterioration in the competitiveness of Austrian tourism and the effects of the international cycle. Thus, the drop in the number of nights

Table 1. **Demand and output**

Percentage change from previous year, constant 1983 prices

	1982-91 average	1992	1993	1994[1]
Private consumption	2.7	1.9	0.2	2.4
Government consumption	1.4	2.4	3.0	3.0
Gross fixed investment	2.9	1.3	−2.1	5.2
Construction	2.5	5.1	2.2	4.0
Machinery and equipment	3.5	−3.6	−8.2	7.0
Change in stocks[2]	0.1	−0.1	0.1	0.7
Total domestic demand	**2.6**	**1.8**	**0.1**	**3.9**
Exports of goods and services	5.2	2.8	−1.0	3.8
of which: Goods	6.7	1.1	−1.0	6.4
Imports of goods and services	5.4	2.6	−0.6	6.0
of which: Goods	5.7	1.4	−0.2	5.9
Foreign balance[2]	0.1	0.6	−0.1	−1.1
Gross domestic product	**2.5**	**1.8**	**−0.1**	**2.8**
Memorandum items:				
GDP price deflator	3.7	4.2	3.6	3.0
Private consumption deflator	3.2	3.9	3.5	2.9
Standardised unemployment rate	3.5	3.6	4.2	4.4[3]

1. Estimates.
2. Change as a per cent of GDP in the previous period.
3. Actual figure.
Source: WIFO; OECD.

spent by foreign tourists in 1993 was heavily concentrated on tourists from countries where the exchange rate had depreciated against the schilling, while the further fall in 1994 seems to be mainly accounted for by German tourists, which may be seen in the context of the weakness in the real income of German households.[1]

The strength of business investment early in the current recovery implies that the upward shift in the investment ratio which could be observed around the late 1980s, has been maintained through the recent cycle (Diagram 3). The already high ratio of capital stock per worker in the Austrian business sector is thus likely to have risen further.[2] The early investment recovery may partly have reflected tax incentives, with the pre-announced halving of the investment tax allowance taking effect from April 1994. Indeed, investment in machinery and equipment grew at a ''freak'' annual rate of more than 50 per cent in the first quarter of 1994, only to contract significantly in the second quarter. However, by the third quarter of 1994 a third of firms surveyed in business surveys reported that they were producing at full capacity, and the strong rise in industrial produc-

Diagram 3. **BUSINESS SECTOR GROWTH AND INVESTMENT**

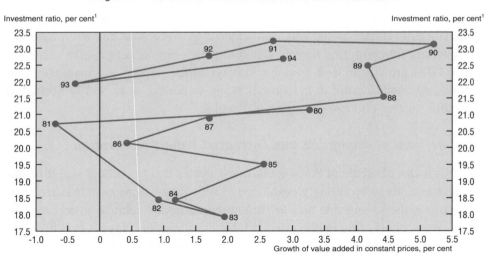

1.   Calculated as business investment/value added, in constant prices.
Source: OECD, Analytic Data Base.

tion of investment goods into the third quarter suggested that the investment set-back in the previous quarter was only temporary (Diagram 4, Panel A). More-over, the positive result of the June referendum concerning EU membership may well have unleashed some pent-up investment projects towards the end of the year.

Residential investment remained relatively buoyant through the recession and has continued to grow during the recovery, the value of housing orders being some 18 per cent higher at the end of the first quarter of 1994 than a year earlier. Despite their rise through 1994, long-term interest rates remain lower than in the late 1980s and early 1990s. However, given the small role that market interest rates play for housing credit,[3] it is not clear that the buoyancy of residential investment was more than partially due to lower interest rates. Housing support programmes, both ordinary (*Wohnbauförderungsprogramme*) and special (*Sonderwohnbauprogramme*), organised by the Länder expanded strongly.[4] Moreover, there may have been an element of correction following the drop in housing investment over the period 1980-92, when the number of dwellings produced was approximately halved. As a sign that construction firms expect the recovery to continue, they have (according to business surveys) been revising up their own investment plans.

Contrary to the experience in many other countries, stockbuilding appears to have moderated rather than amplified the cycle up to the middle of 1994. A build-up of stocks occurred as the economy entered the recession and even over the four quarters following the trough, stockbuilding gave no net positive contribu-tion to GDP growth. Indeed, business surveys in the mining and manufacturing sectors continued to point to inventories being somewhat in excess of normal in the fourth quarter of 1994 (Diagram 4, Panel C).

More hesitant consumption and increased import penetration

It is a characteristic of Austrian business cycles that household real disposa-ble income tends to be strongly cushioned against fluctuations in output and that, furthermore, the saving rate acts to smooth consumption relative to income.[5] In the recovery phase, this implies that private consumption plays a less dynamic role than in some other countries. Hence, despite a boost to disposable incomes of some Sch 13 billion, corresponding to about 1 per cent of consumption, arising from the second phase of the 1993/94 tax reform, household real disposable

Diagram 4. THE RECOVERY IN THE BUSINESS SECTOR

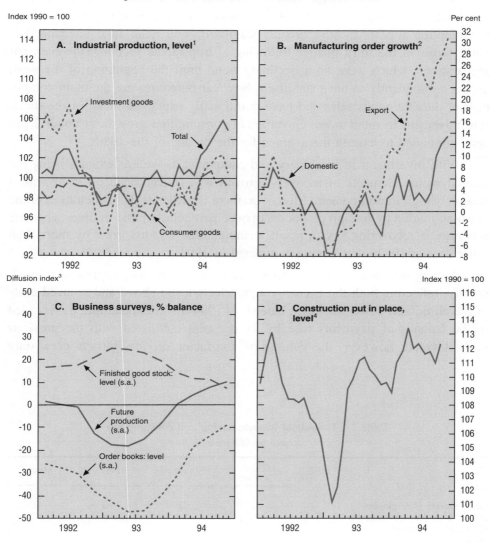

1. 3-month moving average.
2. New orders inflows, percentage change from year ago, 3-month moving average.
3. Balance of positive – negative replies.
4. Total value of work put in place deflated by the index of residential construction costs. 3-month moving average, seasonally adjusted.
Source: Austrian Institute for Economic Research (WIFO) and OECD, *Main Economic Indicators.*

income grew only in line with GDP in 1994 and, in addition, the saving rate rose by about 1 percentage point (Table 2). Indeed, since the first quarter of 1994 consumption appears to have broadly stagnated, with retail sales unchanged in value terms in the third quarter following a drop in the second. However, car registrations, which were on a declining trend until the beginning of the year, appear subsequently to have stabilised. New car purchases are the main component of durable goods sales and have traditionally explained much of the short-run movement in retail sales. Government consumption growth, at about 3 per cent, continued to exceed the average for the decade of the 1980s.

With investment in machinery and equipment as well as exports being the most dynamic elements of recovery, growth was concentrated on areas with a relatively high import content. Moreover, there is evidence that penetration of the Austrian market by foreign producers may be particularly rapid in times when the economy is recovering.[6] As a result, manufactured imports grew by more than 8 per cent in 1994, after having contracted in 1993.

Among non-factor service imports, tourism expenditure continued to grow rapidly, reflecting both the exchange rate effects noted above and reduced costs of travel, notably lower air fares. Indeed, in 1994 travel expenditure as recorded in the balance of payments rose by 11 per cent compared with the previous year.[7] Overall, however, the volume of non-factor service imports grew only

Table 2. **Household income, saving and consumption**

Annual growth, per cent

	1982-91 average	1992	1993	1994[1]
Compensation of employees	5.7	7.3	4.3	4.0
Income from property and other	9.8	5.1	-3.4	5.7
Net transfers received	6.7	6.7	9.3	9.6
Direct taxes	6.2	10.1	3.2	1.4
Disposable income	6.7	4.2	2.7	6.5
Consumption	6.0	5.9	3.7	5.4
Saving rate, per cent of disposable income	11.0	12.5	11.7	12.7

1. Estimates.
Source: WIFO; OECD.

modestly as expenditure on items other than travel stagnated. Expenditure on some items such as non-distributed services[8] declined sharply.

Production

As a result of the cyclical pattern described above, GDP expanded strongly in the first quarter of 1994, by about 5 to 6 per cent (s.a.a.r), but subsequently slowed significantly, resulting in a yearly growth rate of about 2¾ per cent. The recent cyclical pattern of GDP has to a large extent paralleled that of Germany. Indeed, there is evidence that the link between Austrian and German GDP growth has become increasingly close and even contemporaneous.[9] This is most likely the result of the increased importance of Germany as an export market for Austria, the role of Austrian industry as a supplier to German industry coupled with the increased leanness of inventories, as well as the direct influence of German monetary policy on Austrian interest rates.

The sectoral pattern of recovery has reflected the demand pattern, with construction and manufacturing being the most dynamic sectors (Table 3). Within the manufacturing sector, the relative improvement has been most pronounced in investment-goods-producing firms, which however had suffered most

Table 3. **Output by sector**

Percentage change from previous period, constant 1983 prices

	1982-91 average	1992	1993	1994[1]
Agriculture	1.2	−3.0	1.5	4.0
Mining, manufacturing and utilities	2.7	−0.2	−3.6	3.7
Construction	1.1	5.4	2.1	3.5
Services	2.9	2.7	1.4	2.4
Trade, transport and tourism	3.4	2.2	−0.2	1.8
Other private services	3.3	3.3	2.2	2.9
Public sector	1.5	2.6	3.2	3.0
Gross domestic product	2.5	1.8	−0.1	2.8

1. Estimates.
Source: WIFO; OECD.

from the recession, and in firms relying on exports (Diagram 4, Panels A and B). Nevertheless, it was only in July 1994 that industrial production reached its previous peak, recorded in May 1992. All segments of the construction sector have expanded through the recent cycle, overall volume growth averaging about 4 per cent in 1994, with an exceptional spike in the first quarter, substantially due to the approaching expiry of the temporary hike in the investment tax allowance in combination with extraordinary weakness a year earlier.

Output developments in the service sectors have been less cyclical. Trade and tourism sectors have, as discussed above, suffered from weak demand while growth in other service sectors has continued to be largely unaffected by the cyclical fluctuations in the industrial and construction sectors.

Early recovery in the labour market

Productivity per person has usually shown strong pro-cyclical variations in Austria and may broadly have conformed to this pattern in the current recovery. For the business sector as a whole, employment is estimated to have grown by $1/4$ to $1/2$ per cent in 1994 whereas output is likely to have expanded by about $2^3/4$ to 3 per cent. Reflecting its fall during 1993, employment in industry was on average somewhat weaker than in 1993, having been almost 6 per cent lower in the first quarter of 1994 than in the previous year, but stabilising in the course of the year (Diagram 5, Panel A). Productivity rose strongly in industry, in the first half by more than 8 per cent (year-on-year) on a per person basis – almost in line with developments in Germany – but slowing in the course of the year. Part of the explanation for this strong productivity performance was a rise in average hours worked, up by almost 3 per cent in the first half. In construction, employment expanded robustly, growing by 6 to 7 per cent (year-on-year) in the exceptional first quarter, although subsequent improvement was modest. Overall, with employment in services, and particularly the government sector, rising slowly, overall employment is likely to have expanded by $1/2$ per cent during 1994 as a whole (Table 4).

The stabilisation of the labour market was reflected in the number of unfilled vacancies, which reached a trough in the fourth quarter of 1993 and subsequently remained broadly unchanged (Diagram 5, Panel B). The unemployment rate peaked in the second quarter of 1993, only one quarter after the GDP trough, but

Diagram 5. **EMPLOYMENT, UNEMPLOYMENT AND WAGES**

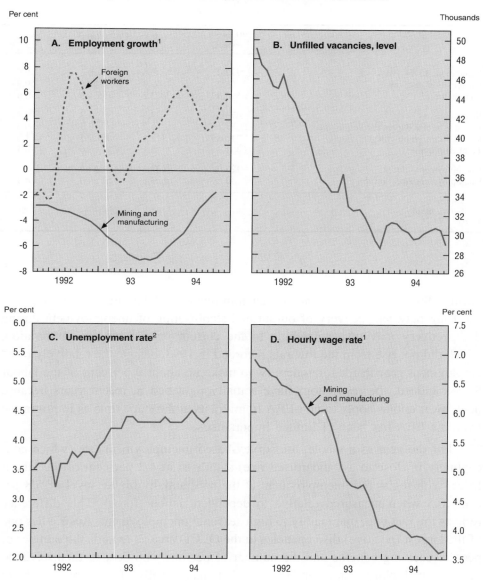

1. Yearly growth rate, 3-month moving average.
2. Survey-based.
Source: WIFO and OECD, *Main Economic Indicators.*

13

Table 4. **Labour supply and demand**

Annual growth, per cent

	1991 level (thousands)	1992	1993	1994[1]
Population, 15-64 years	5 272.0	0.6	0.6	0.6
Participation rate, level	68.2	69.3	69.8	69.8
Labour force[2]	3 596.3	2.2	1.3	0.6
Self-employed	473.5	3.2	5.3	0.4
Business sector dependent employment	2 287.1	1.7	−0.3	0.3
Public sector employment	710.6	2.4	0.5	1.0
Total employment	3 471.3	2.1	0.6	0.5
Unemployment,[2] level	125.0	132.3	157.4	162.7
Unemployment rate,[2] level	3.5	3.6	4.2	4.4

1. Estimates.
2. Survey based.
Source: OECD.

during 1994 there has been no further improvement (Diagram 5, Panel C). The short lag between recovery of output and stabilisation of unemployment during this recovery may owe something to the current restrictions on immigration, which did not rise from the low rate recorded in 1993, despite the relatively rapid employment growth for foreigners (who make up about 9 per cent of the labour force). Indeed, the restrictions have actually tightened in recent years because new lower quotas apply to non-EEA immigrants at the same time as immigration from the EEA has been of limited importance.

For the year as a whole, the survey-based unemployment rate (which conceptually is close to a standardised rate) stabilised at 4.3 per cent of the labour force, with registered unemployment at the substantially higher level of 5.8 per cent (6.5 when measured relative to dependent labour force). This difference reflects the fact that, due mainly to high seasonal unemployment, Austria has one of the largest (positive) discrepancies in the OECD area as regards the number of people receiving benefits and the number of persons who declare themselves to be actively looking for a job.[10] Given that many spells of unemployment are relatively short, the total number of persons affected by unemployment in the course of 1994 is expected to have been close to ³/₄ million or 20 per cent of the labour force.[11]

14

Stubborn inflation

The 1994 wage round (negotiated in autumn 1993) was conducted against the background of apparently rising unemployment. For the pace-setting metal industry it gave a rise in average effective wages (Ist-Löhne) of 2.8 per cent, with an increase in basic wages of 3.8 per cent. An original feature was an opening clause, allowing companies in distress to negotiate directly with their workforce on lower wage increases than stipulated by the agreement. The agreement was seen as a contribution to the "solidarity pact", subsequently endorsed by the social partners, in which the various territorial authorities agreed to refrain from raising taxes and to prevent administered prices from rising faster than general inflation. Moreover, all available means (including competition policy, price and cartel law) were to be used to dampen price movements outside the public sector.

In the event, wage increases broadly followed the agreed path (Diagram 5, Panel D). With robust productivity growth, this implied falling unit labour costs in manufacturing and a sharp slowdown for the private sector as a whole (Table 5). However, inflation fell much more slowly than envisaged under the "pact" due, mainly, to widening profit margins, higher indirect taxes and administered prices as well as higher rents (Diagram 6, Panel A). Rents have continued to grow at rates in excess of 6 per cent and, in conformity with the usual pattern, the contribution of profit margins to inflation increased as that of other components decreased (Diagram 6, Panel B). As a result, disinflation in Austria pro-

Table 5. **Wages and prices**

Annual growth, per cent

	1982-91 average	1992	1993	1994[1]
Hourly earnings, manufacturing	5.1	5.9	4.6	4.3
Unit labour costs, manufacturing	0.7	3.1	0.2	−2.2
Compensation per employee, total business sector	5.2	5.7	4.5	3.1
Unit labour costs, business sector	3.1	5.4	4.3	1.2
GDP deflator	3.7	4.2	3.6	3.0
Private consumption deflator	3.2	3.9	3.5	2.9

1. Estimates.
Source: WIFO; OECD.

15

Diagram 6. **INFLATION**

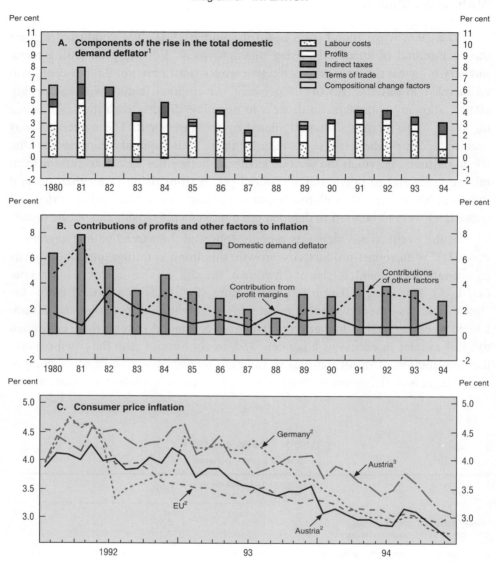

1. See Technical Annex of the *1993/94 OECD Economic Survey of Austria* for the decomposition of the total domestic deflator.
2. Growth over 12 months.
3. CPI excluding food and energy, growth over 12 months.
Source: OECD, *National Accounts* and *Main Economic Indicators.*

16

ceeded at a significantly slower pace than in Germany, although Austria maintained a relative inflation performance around the EU average (Diagram 6, Panel C).

With the recovery becoming increasingly established, the wage round for 1995 in the metal industry was concluded rapidly, with a result close to union demands. Basic wages were raised by 3.8 per cent, as in the previous round, but with a minimum increase of Sch 600, bringing the rise to about 6 per cent for the lowest wages. Average effective wages (Ist-Löhne) were to increase by 3.5 per cent, slightly more than in the previous round. In addition, a one-off conjunctural bonus of Sch 2 000 was granted, with the effect that average earnings growth in the metal industry will be about 4.2 per cent. The new agreement does not include an opening clause. The experience with the previous clause was that relatively few firms made use of it. The subsequent agreement in the distribution sector implies slightly lower average wage increases, with basic wages raised by 3.6 per cent. No changes have been made to wage supplements (the difference between the basic wage and Ist-Löhne), which for the sub-sectors and areas (such as Vienna) where these supplements are large is likely to entail effective wage increases as low as 2$^{1}/_{2}$ per cent. In the public sector, contractual wage increases of 2.9 per cent together with the introduction of a pay reform and structural effects related, *inter alia*, to strongly seniority-related pay scales may combine to raise average wages by about 4 per cent.

Deteriorating external balance

Since 1990 the current account balance has been moving gradually towards deficit, a trend which continued in 1994, with the deficit ending up at Sch 22 billion, or 1 per cent of GDP (Table 6). With imports of goods growing more strongly than exports, and with the terms of trade weakening slightly, the trade balance is estimated to have deteriorated by nearly Sch 19 billion. Transit trade remained in significant surplus, despite Austria's transformation from being an intermediary for East-West trade to being increasingly one for intra-eastern European trade in the wake of the break-up of Comecon.[12] The other main contribution to a weakening current account came from a lower net revenue from tourism which, as described above, was caused both by increased Austrian tourism abroad and by fewer visits by foreign tourists in Austria.

17

Table 6. **Current account of the balance of payments**

Billion schillings

	1990	1991	1992	1993	1994 [1]
Goods and services	13.7	1.0	10.0	4.5	−13.8
Merchandise	−90.2	−112.9	−106.4	−97.7	−116.4
Exports	466.1	479.0	487.6	467.2	512.5
Imports	556.2	591.9	593.9	564.9	628.9
Transit trade	10.8	10.1	9.7	11.0	10.5
Travel	64.7	74.8	67.4	61.4	43.7
Exports	152.4	161.2	159.6	157.5	150.3
Imports	87.8	86.3	93.2	96.1	106.6
Investment income	−11.0	−17.6	−13.1	−11.5	−10.2
Unclassified goods or services	30.7	36.3	30.5	14.4	24.3
Other items	8.7	10.1	21.9	27.0	34.2
Transfers	−0.0	−0.2	−11.6	−12.7	−8.4
Official	−2.1	−2.3	−5.4	−6.8	−7.1
Private	2.1	2.1	−6.2	−5.9	−1.3
Current account	13.6	−1.0	−1.6	−8.2	−22.3

1. Provisional.
Source: Austrian National Bank.

The rising deficit on the current account has no normative significance *per se*, since an external deficit would only be of concern if it reflected excessive domestic consumption caused by distorted saving and investment decisions. In fact, the 1994 rise in the Austrian deficit reflects a rise in investment which was not fully matched by higher domestic saving (Diagram 7). Both saving and investment are at relatively high levels in Austria and the domestic saving deficiency, though rising, remains comparatively low. What is a cause for concern, however, is the fact that the domestic counterpart of the external deficit over recent years is to be found in a rising public sector deficit; the private sector has actually improved its financial position since 1990, although this trend came to a halt in 1994.

Long-term net capital inflows far exceeded the current account deficit in 1993 but diminished substantially in the course of 1994 (Table 7). Both foreign direct investment in Austria and foreigners' portfolio investment in Austrian shares continued to expand significantly in 1994. However, foreign purchases of Austrian bonds declined through the year and eventually turned into reselling

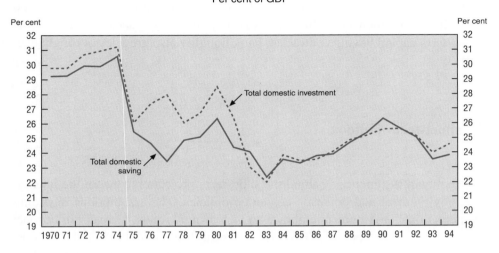

Diagram 7. **SAVING AND INVESTMENT**
Per cent of GDP

Source: OECD, *National Accounts.*

Table 7. **Capital account of the balance of payments**
Billion schillings

	1991	1992	1993	1994 [1]
Direct investment	−10.9	−10.2	−5.7	0.7
Austrian abroad	15.0	20.6	17.1	14.3
Foreign in Austria	4.2	10.3	11.4	15.0
Portfolio investment in shares and investment certificates	0.9	1.0	7.5	6.4
Austrian abroad	1.5	1.5	6.3	8.8
Foreign in Austria	2.4	2.5	13.8	15.2
Portfolio investment in fixed-interest securities	12.2	37.7	92.0	−3.8
Austrian abroad	18.4	27.7	14.0	38.6
Foreign in Austria	30.6	65.4	106.0	34.9
Loans	−30.7	−13.5	1.4	0.8
To foreigners	31.6	13.1	2.0	8.7
To residents	0.9	−0.4	3.4	9.4
Long-term capital	−24.4	7.9	75.3	10.8
Short-term capital	24.8	13.2	−34.9	21.2

1. Provisional.
Source: Austrian National Bank.

whilst Austrian purchases of foreign bonds increased, as the differential between Austrian and German interest rates virtually disappeared and foreign investors no longer diversified their portfolios into Austria at the same pace. With the inflow of long-term capital having contracted, bank liquidity also grew less strongly than in 1993.

The short-term outlook

The main assumptions behind the short-term projection concern the international environment and domestic economic policies. The assumptions regarding the international environment embrace an increasingly robust recovery in Europe, where growth may settle at 3 to 3¼ per cent from mid-1995 and onwards, together with a slowdown in the United States. Central and eastern European countries which are an important market for Austria, may experience an acceleration of imports over the period to 1996. For Austria, these projections imply that export market growth is likely to remain in the range of 7 to 8 per cent attained in the second half of 1994 (Table 8). Underlying the projections are technical assumptions of unchanged exchange rates as of 1 March 1995 and an average OECD import price of oil which in real terms remains at the level of $15.60 per barrel prevailing in the second half of 1994.

Since the focus of Austrian monetary policy will continue to be on maintaining an unchanged exchange rate between the schilling and the Deutschemark, and short-term interest rates in Germany are projected to remain stable before rising through 1996, a similar pattern is projected for Austrian short-term interest rates. The slight negative short-term spread, which prevailed for part of 1993 and 1994, was caused by abundant liquidity in the Austrian financial system due to autonomous capital inflows and since these are not assumed to continue, the spread is unlikely to persist. Long-term yields are also projected to follow a path similar to German rates, despite a continued adverse inflation differential. Concerning fiscal policy, the path of fiscal consolidation implies an underlying improvement in the cyclically-adjusted general government budget balance of about ½ to ¾ per cent of GDP in both 1995 and 1996, exclusive of EU contributions (see Part II).

Table 8. **Economic projections to 1996**

Percentage change from previous year, constant 1983 prices

	1993	1994[1]	1995[2]	1996[2]
Private consumption	0.2	2.4	2.0	2.5
Government consumption	3.0	3.0	2.0	1.0
Gross fixed investment	−2.1	5.2	5.8	5.6
Construction	2.2	4.0	4.0	4.0
Machinery and equipment	−8.2	7.0	8.5	8.0
Change in stocks[3]	0.1	0.7	0.1	0.0
Total domestic demand	0.1	3.9	3.1	3.0
Exports of goods and services	−1.0	3.8	5.1	5.3
Imports of goods and services	−0.6	6.0	5.7	6.0
Foreign balance[3]	−0.1	−1.1	−0.4	−0.5
Gross domestic product	−0.1	2.8	2.7	2.6
Memorandum items:				
Private consumption deflator	3.5	2.9	2.3	2.8
GDP price deflator	3.6	3.0	2.8	2.9
Total employment	0.6	0.5	0.6	0.8
Unemployment rate, level[4]	4.2	4.4	4.3	4.2
Household saving ratio, level	11.7	12.7	12.5	11.9
Export market growth	−4.1	7.4	8.4	8.4
Short-term interest rate	7.2	5.0	5.3	6.0
Long-term interest rate	6.6	6.7	7.3	7.2
General government budget balance, per cent of GDP	−4.1	−4.0	−4.6	−3.9
Current balance, per cent of GDP	−0.5	−1.0	−1.3	−1.5

1. Estimates as of March 1995.
2. OECD projections updated to March 1995.
3. Change as a per cent of GDP in the previous period.
4. Standardised definition (survey based).
Source: WIFO; OECD.

The effects of EU accession

EU accession is likely to have important, but not easily quantifiable, effects on business sentiment and investment, as well as more long-term effects on competition and economic efficiency in a wider sense (this is discussed in more detail in Part IV). More immediately, it affects the short-term projection directly and significantly in three areas: inflation, the budget and the external balance. The most important effect on inflation arises because, on average, prices of agricultural products under the CAP are about 23 per cent lower than the prices hitherto prevailing in Austria.[13] The corresponding reduction in prices of food and beverages paid by consumers has been calculated at around 5 per cent,[14] and

21

assuming that about half of this effect is passed on to consumers immediately, the effect on the CPI could be around $1/2$ percentage point (food and beverages having a weight of about 20 per cent). In addition to this effect, lower average customs duties in the EU will imply a slight reduction in import prices (estimated at around $1/4$ per cent), but in the likely event that increases in duty will be more fully passed on than reductions, the net impact on consumer prices is likely to be negligible.[15]

The net negative impact of EU accession on the general government budget is estimated at around Sch 34 billion (1.4 per cent of GDP) in 1995, including both payments to the EU and compensation payments to the Austrian agricultural sector (for further details, see next chapter). Austria's budget contribution will enter as a minus in the external account, but direct EU payments to the private sector will offset more than half this amount, making for a net payment of approximately Sch 12 billion, or $1/2$ per cent of GDP.

The outlook

The demand projections point to a continuation of the export- and investment-led recovery, with private and public consumption lagging, due in part to fiscal consolidation. Thus, exports of goods will be broadly dependent on market growth, but services exports could lag, with structural problems in the tourism sector being a drag on growth. Business investment is likely to remain buoyant, with profitability set to rise with capacity utilisation and little negative impact likely to arise from higher long-term interest rates. Similarly, residential investment may continue to recover, given an expected stepping-up of residential construction programmes operated by the Länder.

With cuts being imposed in transfer programmes, household disposable incomes could expand more slowly than in 1994, the growth in real disposable incomes being projected to be almost 2 per cent in both 1995 and 1996. A lower saving rate may partly offset the impact of weak income growth on private consumption, with household sentiment likely to be favourably influenced by rising employment and decisive action to correct the fiscal imbalance. Overall, total domestic demand could expand at a rate of around 3 per cent, with GDP growing marginally more slowly.

With output growing in excess of potential (estimated to be growing at $2 1/4$ per cent), unemployment is projected to fall further. But the drop could be muted by pro-cyclical productivity and labour-force growth. The implication of the 1995 round is that wage disinflation may have come to an end, but no major re-acceleration of wages is foreseen within the projection period. This is due, in part, to the slowdown in price inflation as a result of EU accession. Nevertheless, a pick-up in unit labour costs may contribute to a slight rebound of inflation

Net transfers abroad are set to increase as a result of EU accession. The external balance could thus weaken in 1995, staying broadly constant in 1996 at a level slightly above 1 per cent of GDP.

II. Macroeconomic and structural policies

Overview

Monetary conditions have eased in line with those in Germany, the parity of Austrian and German interest rates testifying to the continued credibility of the fixed exchange-rate policy. However, fiscal policy has been under strain and is a potentially destabilising influence unless underlying expenditure trends are corrected. The goal of achieving the Maastricht convergence criteria will require strict budgetary consolidation. Measures to this effect have been announced, but the task would be easier if the trend to structural reform were reinforced, particularly with respect to the efficiency of public sector management and to privatisation.

Monetary and exchange rate policy

An anchor for inflation expectations

Since the early 1980s, Austrian monetary policy has focused on the exchange-rate link to Germany as providing the most reliable framework for stabilising business expectations. This policy has been very successful both in gaining widespread acceptance within Austria and acquiring a large degree of international credibility. These aspects are mutually dependent: the credibility of the fixed exchange-rate strategy has been enhanced because there is no serious domestic opinion pressing for change, while the strategy has become so widely accepted because its credibility implied a relatively favourable interest rate premium. Moreover, although German unification forced monetary policy into a restrictive stance in the early stages of the recession, the growing integration of Germany and Austria means that the setting of interest rates implied by the exchange-rate link has become increasingly appropriate from the point of view of macroeconomic management.[16] The entry of Austria into the European Monetary System and its Exchange Rate Mechanism (on 9 January 1995) can thus be seen as an extension of a stability-oriented monetary policy which had already been internationally established, the exchange rate strategy remaining essentially unaltered.

Diagram 8 illustrates the evolution of the Austrian exchange rate *vis-à-vis* the Deutschemark since 1981, together with the cumulative interest rate premium needed to maintain parity with the Deutschemark. Over that period, Austria has had virtually no premium built into its interest rates, particularly at the short end, compared to Germany. The reasons for Austria's favourable performance in this regard are complex, but the role of inflation, and particularly inflation expectations, in establishing and maintaining credibility has probably been crucial. In the mid-1980s, Austria experienced a period of inflation in excess of German rates and, with a short lag, the interest differentials went up, particularly at the long end. Inflation in the Netherlands never rose above German levels and interest differentials remained negligible, while the interest premium paid by Belgium and Denmark only began to fall after the inflation differential *vis-à-vis* Germany was eliminated. However, the fact that the long-term differential in these economies continues to be positive even so, means that other factors, such as the budget deficit, play a role here, and point to the potential dangers involved for Austria if the current and prospective budget deficit is not contained.

Recent developments

Following the trend of German rates, Austrian short-term interest rates have fallen since the autumn of 1992, levelling off since May 1994. Since 1992, short-term market rates in Austria have generally been slightly below similar rates in Germany (Diagram 9). Moreover, in the period since German official rates began falling in the autumn of 1992, the Austrian National Bank has been able to reduce Austrian official interest rates ahead of similar German rates. Subsequent to the May 1994 cut, however, German and Austrian discount rates have been identical at 4½ per cent. Nevertheless, the rate on the National Bank's short-term open market operations (GOMEX) has since remained some 10 to 20 basis points below the German repo rate. For long-term bond yields, the spread between Austrian and German rates has also been virtually eliminated for directly comparable bonds. As a result, long-term interest rates have closely followed German

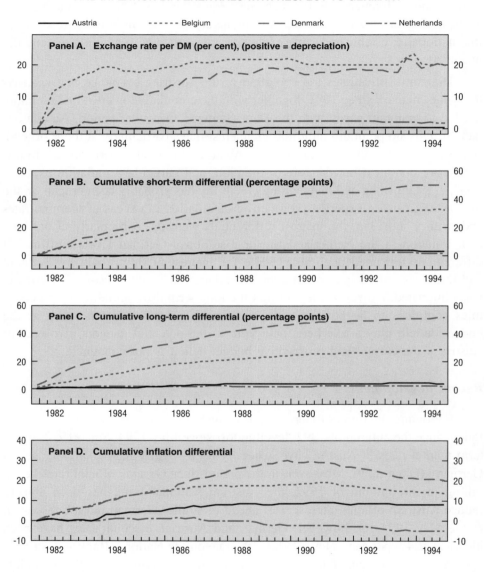

Diagram 8. **CURRENCY MOVEMENTS, INTEREST RATE SPREADS AND INFLATION DIFFERENTIALS WITH RESPECT TO GERMANY**[1]

——— Austria ・・・・・ Belgium — — Denmark —・— Netherlands

Panel A. Exchange rate per DM (per cent), (positive = depreciation)

Panel B. Cumulative short-term differential (percentage points)

Panel C. Cumulative long-term differential (percentage points)

Panel D. Cumulative inflation differential

1. Exchange rate changes are calculated with respect to Q4 1981. Interest rates are cumulated from this date as well. For example since Q4 1981, the Austrian Schilling has remained stable with respect to the DM and the sum of short-term interest differentials has been about 2 percentage points.
Source: OECD.

26

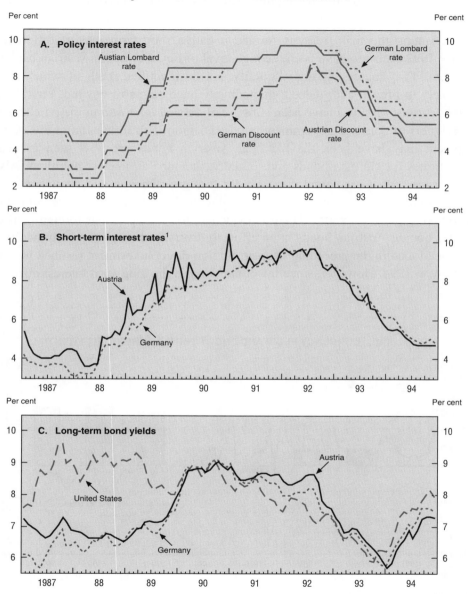

Diagram 9. **INTEREST RATE DEVELOPMENTS**

Per cent

A. Policy interest rates

Austian Lombard rate

German Lombard rate

German Discount rate

Austrian Discount rate

10 · 8 · 6 · 4 · 2

1987 · 88 · 89 · 90 · 91 · 92 · 93 · 94

Per cent

B. Short-term interest rates[1]

Austria

Germany

10 · 8 · 6 · 4

1987 · 88 · 89 · 90 · 91 · 92 · 93 · 94

Per cent

C. Long-term bond yields

Austria

United States

Germany

10 · 9 · 8 · 7 · 6

1987 · 88 · 89 · 90 · 91 · 92 · 93 · 94

1. Call money.
Source: OECD, *Financial Statistics.*

27

rates, rising by some 150 basic points since the trough in early 1994 but stabilising in the latter part of 1994.

Among the main reasons for the negative short-term interest differential since 1992 seems to have been the high level of liquidity in the Austrian banking system. Two sources of high liquidity can be identified, both of which seem unlikely to prevail and, indeed, may already have begun to unwind. First, since 1992 currency inflows have been substantial, related *inter alia* to the purchase by foreigners of Austrian government bonds (Diagram 10). Influential in this development may have been the fact that Austrian bonds are now seen as near-substitutes for German bonds and, initially, included an interest premium. Also, the process of deregulating cross-border foreign exchange and capital transactions was only completed in November 1991, making the market more liquid and prompting portfolio shifts. There is evidence, for example, that foreign pension funds bought Austrian bonds in an effort to diversify their portfolio. In addition, as mentioned in the preceding chapter, foreign direct investment resulted in a net inflow in 1994. However, since the elimination of the long-term interest differen-

Diagram 10. **CURRENCY FLOW AND SHORT-TERM INTEREST DIFFERENTIAL**

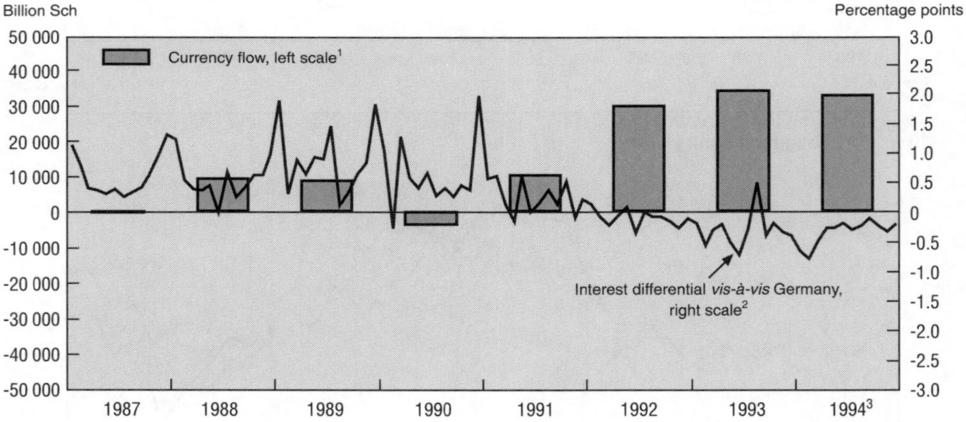

1. Change in official exchange reserve.
2. Call money rates.
3. Year to end-October for currency flow.
Source : Austrian National Bank and OECD, *Financial Statistics.*

tial in early 1994, net foreign currency inflows appear to have dried up and exchange reserves have been slightly declining since mid-1994.

The second reason for the high level of liquidity has been the relative weakness of domestic borrowing from the banking system. In the period 1985-91, total bank credits to the non-bank sector rose at an average rate of 8.7 per cent but in the period from end-1991 to December 1994 growth was only about 5 per cent. With the recovery becoming increasingly established, credit demand has begun to rise. Indeed, among the first signs of this happening may be that total bank credit expanded by almost 60 per cent more in the course of the first nine months of 1994 compared with the similar period of 1993. Comparing the same periods, bank acquisition of assets abroad declined by 27 per cent and their foreign liabilities rose more than twice as fast, implying that banks no longer acquired foreign assets on a net basis – previously a main outlet for surplus liquidity.

The developments in the yield curve have had repercussions on the growth of monetary aggregates. The steepening of the curve since autumn 1992 has reduced the attractiveness of savings deposits relative to bonds, helping to explain the moderate growth of M3 of around 4 per cent annually since 1992. However, M1 has been buoyant, reflecting an increased liquidity preference as a result of lower short-term interest rates, leading to a shift from savings to sight deposits. In addition, in the course of 1994, uncertainties concerning the development of long-term interest rates led to some temporary "parking" of funds, boosting M1 growth to 12 per cent in the first half of the year. With the pick-up in economic activity throughout 1994, there are some signs that M3 growth may be reviving – it reached 5 per cent over the twelve months to December – and M1 growth remained high in the second half of 1994, despite firmer long-term interest rates.

Fiscal policy

Recent budgetary developments

For the second year running, the initial estimate of the Federal budget deficit was exceeded in 1994 (Table 9). On a "cash" basis (excluding the effects of reserves movements and other "double entry" items), the budget overrun was

Table 9. **The Federal budget**

Cash basis; in billions of schillings

	1992 Outturn	1993 Outturn	1994 Budget	1994 Outturn[1]	1995 Budget
Revenue	**559.3**	**562.3**	**586.1**	**581.3**	**590.0**
Taxes before revenue sharing	509.1	512.8	531.1	524.5	528.0
Wage tax	134.3	139.2	138.0	134.8	150.5
Taxes on other income and profits	74.4	66.3	64.0	57.0	54.3
Value-added tax	173.0	176.0	196.0	202.6	189.0
Major excise taxes[2]	37.8	37.0	38.5	39.3	45.5
Other taxes	89.6	94.3	94.6	90.8	88.7
Minus tax-sharing transfers	168.9	173.7	169.6	166.1	159.0
Minus transfers to EU budget	0	0	0	0	28.1
Taxes after revenue sharing	340.2	339.1	361.4	358.4	340.9
Tax transfers to federal funds	19.2	19.1	19.5	19.3	19.7
Tax-like revenue[3]	66.7	72.2	79.9	79.5	84.0
Federal enterprises	79.0	78.8	63.0	63.9	65.9
Other revenue	54.2	53.1	62.2	60.2	79.5
Expenditure	**618.7**	**665.6**	**680.6**	**681.1**	**709.3**
Wages and salaries	146.5	155.5	133.8	136.5	137.3
Pensions	59.4	63.6	66.0	66.9	49.7
Current expenditure on goods	51.2	62.0	59.6	65.6	67.0
Gross investment	26.8	26.4	24.9	24.3	25.8
Transfer payments	232.1	259.2	288.1	282.3	314.4
Family allowances	52.1	59.3	61.6	62.1	58.3
Unemployment benefits	23.8	31.1	34.9	32.8	33.5
Transfers to the social security	61.2	68.9	72.9	73.4	78.8
Transfers to enterprises	20.0	20.7	34.2	31.5	47.4
Other transfers	75.0	79.3	84.5	82.5	96.4
Interest	74.0	77.6	78.8	78.7	88.1
Other expenditure	28.7	21.3	29.4	26.9	26.9
Net balance	**−59.3**	**−103.3**	**−94.5**	**−99.8**	**−119.2**
(in per cent of GDP)	(2.9)	(4.9)	(4.3)	(4.4)	(5.0)
Memorandum item:					
Net balance, administrative basis	**−66.3**	**−98.2**	**−80.7**	**−104.8**	**−102.2**
(in per cent of GDP)	(3.2)	(4.7)	(3.7)	(4.7)	(4.3)

1. March 1995 estimate.
2. Mineral oil, tobacco and alcohol taxes.
3. Mainly contributions to unemployment insurance and to the fund for family allowances.
Source: Ministry of Finance.

Sch 5½ billion.[17] As current expenditure was, on the whole, close to the original budget,[18] the main reasons for the overrun were to be found on the revenue side. However, unlike 1993 when weaker-than-expected economic activity was a main reason for the budget overrun, activity in 1994 actually turned out stronger than expected. Higher real economic growth (2¾ instead of 1½ per cent), lower unemployment (6½ instead of 7½ per cent on a register base) and higher inflation (3 per cent for the CPI against 2¾ per cent) than anticipated should have made for higher-than-expected tax revenues. But this was more than offset by unanticipated effects of tax reform, and a faster-than-normal write-off of recession-induced income losses in tax declarations. In addition, there was a Sch 7 billion shortfall in privatisation receipts due to delays in the privatisation programme, notably in the sale of Creditanstalt. The net effect was that the federal deficit remained broadly unchanged compared to the 1993 level. With continued stability in the combined surplus in Länder, local government and social security, the overall general government budget deficit likewise remained at around its 1993 level (Table 10).

Table 10. **Net lending of the general government**

National accounts basis, billions of schillings

	1992	1993	1994 [1]	1995 [1]	1996 [1]
Current receipts	**991.1**	**1 029.0**	**1 068.5**	**1 132.3**	**1 192.7**
Total direct taxes	297.8	304.9	293.9	311.7	332.4
Households	246.9	254.9	258.4	274.0	292.1
Business	50.8	50.0	35.5	37.7	40.3
Total indirect taxes	325.8	338.6	364.2	379.5	398.0
Social security and other current transfers received	321.8	342.7	364.4	391.6	411.4
Property and entrepreneurial income	45.7	42.8	46.0	49.5	50.9
Current disbursements	**950.2**	**1 024.4**	**1 073.4**	**1 148.9**	**1 196.5**
Government consumption	377.1	405.6	426.8	447.1	463.5
of which: Wages and salaries	257.8	277.5	288.3	297.8	306.7
Interest on public debt	87.9	93.0	93.7	103.3	111.4
Subsidies	61.2	63.5	64.0	69.0	71.0
Social security outlays and other current transfers paid	424.0	462.3	488.9	529.5	550.6
Capital outlays	**82.4**	**92.0**	**85.1**	**91.3**	**92.7**
Gross investment	67.3	69.3	66.6	70.0	71.7
Net capital transfers paid and other capital transactions	28.9	37.2	33.8	37.3	37.6
less: Consumption of fixed capital	13.8	14.5	15.3	16.0	16.6
Net lending	**−41.6**	**−87.4**	**−90.0**	**−107.9**	**−96.5**
(as a per cent of GDP)	(-2.0)	(-4.1)	(-4.0)	(-4.5)	(-3.9)

1. OECD estimates and projections as of March 1995.
Source: Ministry of Finance; OECD.

Since output growth was a little higher than the estimated growth of potential, the output gap narrowed in 1994, implying a significant rise in the cyclically-adjusted general government budget deficit to around 3 per cent of GDP[19] (Diagram 11, Panel A). This estimate of the structural deficit broadly corresponds to that obtained if changes in inflation are used to define the GDP gap, based on the hypothesis that inflation declines when actual output is lower than potential and increases when it is higher. Thus, declining inflation in both 1993 and 1994 suggests that budget deficits in excess of 4 per cent of GDP included a significant cyclical component which, under simple assumptions, can be quantified at around $1/2$ per cent of GDP in 1994 (Diagram 11, Panel B).[20] With the increase in the cyclically-adjusted deficit in 1994, fiscal policy appears to have been pro-cyclical in the sense that an expansionary fiscal stance was associated with a narrowing output gap. A longer-term perspective on the cyclical stance of fiscal policy is given in Diagram 11, Panel C.

The 1995 budget

Budget developments in 1995 will be affected by a number of decisions already taken and, in some cases, implemented. The business tax reform and the negative income tax for low incomes, both introduced in April 1994, will have a growing impact in 1995 and 1996, which will lead to a drain on tax revenues. In addition, the first phase of a compensation reform for public servants, aimed at stimulating productivity and flexibility at work, will be introduced. In conjunction with ordinary wage increases of 2.9 per cent (see Part I) this could lead to a slight acceleration of the government wage bill. Moreover, a decision has already been reached on raising pensions by 2.8 per cent in 1995, with a promise that if inflation turns out higher than the expected $2^{1/2}$ per cent, it will be taken into account in the 1996 pension negotiations.

Another significant influence on the 1995 budget comes from Austria's EU accession. The government budget will be affected by budget contributions to the EU to the tune of Sch 29 billion in 1995 (Table 11).[21] In addition, farmers and agro-industrial firms will receive adjustment relief, compensation for capital losses on inventories and equalisation payments, amounting to government subsidies of around Sch 13.1 billion in 1995 (and shared by the Federal and Länder governments). On the income side, losses related *inter alia* to lower indirect taxes will be some Sch 1.1 billion. Against this should be set savings on existing

Diagram 11. GOVERNMENT NET LENDING AND THE CYCLICAL POSITION

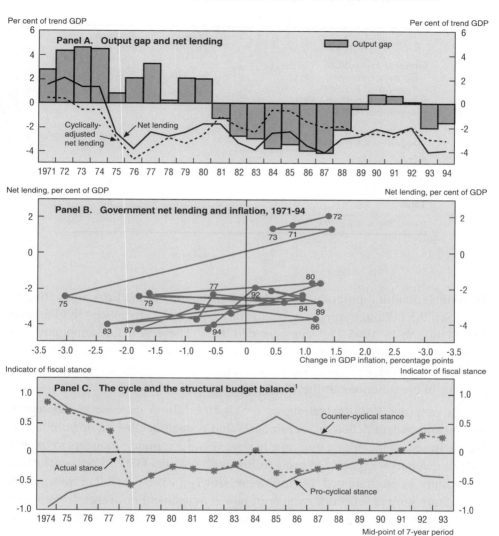

Per cent of trend GDP

Panel A. Output gap and net lending

Output gap

Cyclically-adjusted net lending

Net lending

1971 72 73 74 75 76 77 78 79 80 81 82 83 84 85 86 87 88 89 90 91 92 93 94

Net lending, per cent of GDP

Panel B. Government net lending and inflation, 1971-94

Change in GDP inflation, percentage points

Indicator of fiscal stance

Panel C. The cycle and the structural budget balance[1]

Counter-cyclical stance

Actual stance

Pro-cyclical stance

1974 75 76 77 78 79 80 81 82 83 84 85 86 87 88 89 90 91 92 93

Mid-point of 7-year period

1. The asterisks mark the coefficient b obtained from recursive estimation of the following equation over successive 7-year periods:
   <cyclically adjusted net lending/GDP> = a + b * <output gap>
   The two latest estimates are partly based on projected data. The lines drawn in full represent the 95 per cent confidence interval for the estimated b coefficients. Thus asterisks in the area between the lines represent an average policy stance which was neither significantly pro-cyclical nor counter-cyclical.
   Source: OECD.

Table 11.   **The budgetary impact of EU accession, 1995**

Billion schillings

	EEA/EU	Domestically
Increased expenditure		
EU contributions	29.0	
Equalisation payments		5.3
Inventory adjustment support		3.4
Adjustment support		4.6
Lower revenue		
Indirect tax adjustments		1.1
Budget savings		
EEA contributions	–0.8	
Agricultural market support		–8.7
Total	28.2	5.7

Source: Breuss *et al.* (1994).

Austrian agricultural programmes and on contributions to the EEA amounting to about Sch 9.5 billion, implying net budgetary costs of EU membership of around Sch 34 billion in 1995 (1.4 per cent of GDP). These will fall temporarily in 1996 with the phasing out of inventory compensation and a reduction in adjustment relief, before beginning to rise again as a result of the scheduled general increase in contributions to the EU budget.

In sum, the 1995 budget shows a Sch 19½ billion increase in the central government budget deficit on a cash basis (but a small decline on an administrative basis, which includes a rundown in reserves).[22] Excluding transfers to the EU budget, revenue is expected to grow in line with nominal GDP (6 per cent) while expenditure is programmed to grow more slowly (4 per cent). The restraint in expenditure growth reflects a number of new retrenchment measures, limiting the rise in deficit and setting the stage for budget consolidation in the remainder of the legislative period:

-   Controls on civil service expenditures will reduce overtime and other pay "extras" by 10 per cent, and pension contributions by civil servants will be raised by 1½ per cent, which lowers the required federal subsidisation of the social security funds . These measures come into force on 1 May and amount to Sch 6½ billion in savings. Also, more restrictive rules on early retirement should lead to a rise in the average retirement age of civil servants.

- Family benefits will be reduced by Sch 100 per child per month, and fees for formerly free busing and books for school children will be introduced, reducing federal government subsidies for these items. These measures will result in savings of Sch 2½ billion.
- Unemployment benefits will be curtailed: access to extended maternity leave will be made more difficult; claims for unemployment and welfare benefits will be scrutinised more closely; and special unemployment benefit (family and hardship) supplements, as well as benefits for higher-income workers, will be scaled back. These measures amount to Sch 2½ billion in savings.
- Pension contributions of the self-employed and farmers will be raised, and the liability of the central government to the pension scheme will be lowered from 100.2 to 100 per cent. Budget savings from such measures are estimated at Sch 1½ billion per year.

On the revenue side, moreover, the following additional measures have been introduced:

- The mineral oil tax will be raised by Sch 1.10 per litre for petrol and Sch 0.60 per litre for gasoil, resulting in Sch 5½ billion additional tax revenues (the consumer price index rising by ¼ percentage point as a result).
- A reduction of the business investment allowance from 15 to 9 per cent is expected to raise Sch 3¾ billion.
- A one-time Sch 12 billion loss in VAT receipts on imports from other EU countries, due to a two-month delay in collections, will be effectively offset by Sch 13 billion in planned privatisation receipts.

On a general government basis, the deficit is projected to widen from 4 to 4½ per cent of GDP.

The need for medium-term fiscal consolidation

With a structural general government budget deficit of the order of 3 per cent of GDP in 1994 and a substantial net expenditure increase expected as a result of EU membership and other underlying expenditure pressures on the budget, consolidation has become an imperative if Austria is to meet the Maastricht criteria for participating in Economic and Monetary Union at the earliest stage. As envisaged in the fiscal programme of the new government, the target is to be met mainly through expenditure cuts, although changes in taxation also play a role. But the size of the expenditure cuts needed to comply with these targets will depend on the state of the economic cycle at the time. This will depend importantly on the state of the business cycle abroad – notably in Germany, since, as noted above, movements in the output gap are similar in the two countries. With fiscal consolidation projected to take place in both countries over 1995-96 and monetary policy successful in stabilising inflation, both German and Austrian output would tend to be in the neighbourhood of economic potential by 1997. This is the assumption adopted for the illustrative calculations presented in Diagram 12.

Specifically, Diagram 12 presents projections of the general government deficit and gross debt under three different assumptions about fiscal policy and with a given set of assumptions concerning the general economic environment. The latter include:

- The output gap will be gradually closed by 1997,[23] output growing at its potential rate in 1998. Growth of potential output is put at about 2¼ per cent (see Annex I for details on the derivation of potential output growth).
- The average real interest rate applying to government debt is assumed to be 3¾ per cent, broadly corresponding to the implicit rate observed for 1994.[24]

In the *"policy neutral" scenario*, the budget balance is assumed to be affected by three factors only: the permanent expenditure increase/revenue shortfall due to EU accession, an effect corresponding to 1.4 per cent of GDP in 1995 and 1.1 per cent thereafter; increasing interest payments on the rising debt, and the closing of the initial output gap. The effect of the latter on the budget balance is estimated at around ½ per cent of GDP for a 1 per cent change in the output gap.[25] On the given assumptions, the result is a budget deficit around 5 per cent, with the tendency to rise because of rising interest payments being offset by cyclical revenue gains. Gross government debt increases to 70 per cent of GDP in

Diagram 12. **GOVERNMENT DEFICIT AND DEBT SCENARIOS**

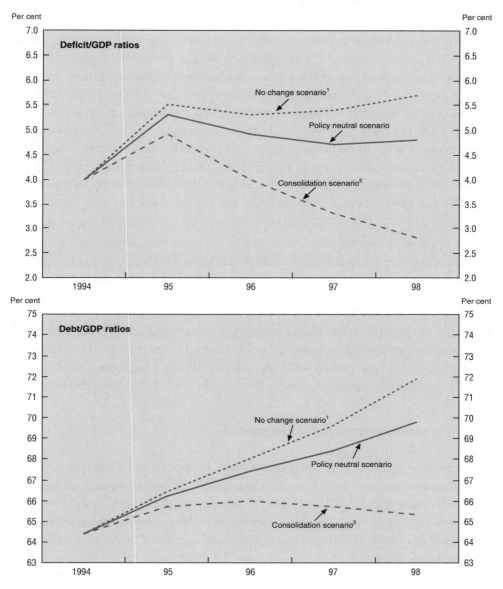

1. Primary structural budget deterioration of 0.20 per cent of GDP annually.
2. Primary structural budget improvement of 0.45 per cent of GDP annually.
Source: OECD.

this scenario which, however, does not take into account any retirement of debt financed through privatisation proceeds.

Underlying budget trends may actually be worse than implied by this scenario. Existing commitments and programmes would, given unchanged tax rates, imply a steady worsening of the primary budget deficit. Indeed, official calculations based on such a technical assumption suggest that the general government budget deficit, net of EU-related expenditure, could deteriorate by about 1 per cent of GDP between 1994 and 1997. The *"no change" scenario* portrays such an outcome where, in addition to the factors affecting the "neutral" scenario, there is an "autonomous" deterioration of the primary budget balance by 0.2 per cent of GDP annually. In this case, the budget deficit rises to close to 6 per cent of GDP and government debt exceeds 70 per cent of GDP.

In order to respect the Maastricht criterion of a 3 per cent deficit by the end of the legislative period, the *"consolidation" scenario* embodies an annual reduction in the primary deficit of about 1/2 per cent of GDP. This is not sufficient to lower public indebtedness below the 60 per cent threshold stipulated by the Maastricht treaty, but the Austrian government has considerable scope for privatisation and corresponding debt retirement and, indeed, plans to use this (see below).[26] In cumulative terms, the budget savings compared with the "neutral" case amount to around 4 1/2 per cent of GDP (or some Sch 100 billion in 1994 prices) over the period 1995-98, while compared with the "no change" scenario such savings amount to more than 6 per cent of GDP (Sch 150 billion).[27]

The new medium-term fiscal programme

The new medium-term programme (Box I) appears somewhat more ambitious than that adopted during the previous period of budgetary consolidation in 1987-92, when the OECD indicator of non-cyclical primary budget balance improved by 1/2 per cent. As shown above, relative to the neutral scenario, the cuts required to meet the Maastricht target in the face of EC accession and higher interest expenditure would amount to some 1 1/2 per cent of GDP per year, over a shorter period. Moreover, the government's own targets are, in fact, more stringent than this. Indeed, the Maastricht targets represent a set of minimal requirements and are, from a point of view of fundamental budget consolidation, not very ambitious, especially when allowance is made for the budget pressures

Box 1. **The new fiscal programme**

The new programme contains a large number of individual elements, with details on a large number of issues still to be worked out in discussions with the social partners. On the expenditure side, overall expenditure targets will be set for the whole legislative period. The main features of the programme are as follows:

– Public sector wage growth will be restricted to what is consistent with budgetary consolidation. The implementation of the public sector wage reform will further restrict the scope for general wage increases. A low rate of wage increase will also affect the growth of pension entitlements in the public sector, which could previously not fall below those of the private-sector pension scheme. Pension contribution of civil servants are to be raised by 1.5 per cent per annum.

– Public sector overtime work will be reduced and the number of posts is to decline by 1 per cent per year.

– Pensions for public servants will be reduced to about 80 per cent of final salary, by changing the pension base to the average of the last five years' salary, gradually rising to fifteen years over the course of the next ten years (possibly to be substituted by other measures).

– All measures applying to public sector employees are also to apply to employees in institutions and enterprises financed through compulsory contributions or subsidies (such as chambers, social security, and the ÖBB).

– Measures will be taken to increase the effective pension age, including stricter control of applications for early and invalidity pensions and cuts in pensions for those who choose early retirement. The pension contributions of the self-employed are to be increased.

– Family grants are to be reduced. Introducing user fees, savings will be made on assistance in connection with transportation to and from school, free school books etc. Contributions from the Länder to family policy will be increased.

– Unemployment insurance contributions will be raised for employers and employees in seasonal sectors (or, alternatively, benefits will be lowered). Abolition of special family allowance in unemployment benefits is to be considered together with various cuts in special benefits (for

older persons and for certain sectors). Alternatively, spreads between benefits under unemployment insurance and assistance are to be increased.

– The number of pupil hours in schools will be reduced and teacher hours raised, while in universities compulsory lessons will be reduced and the supply of different educations will be rationalised.

– Plans are to be prepared for cost savings in the health and care sectors.

– Revenue from a gradual widening of the mineral oil tax to cover other sources of energy is to be used for lowering taxes on labour income.

– Government investment is to be cut and there is to be increased private-sector financing of infrastructure investment.

– Subsidies are to be reduced.

arising from population ageing which will become increasingly acute, as described in last year's *Survey*.

If output grew more rapidly than indicated, and expanded significantly beyond potential, the target for the budget balance could be achieved with fewer expenditure cuts. However this would entail less fiscal restraint in a situation where it might seem needed, involving a slackening in the pace of consolidation which would be exposed during a subsequent downturn. Hence, the scale of the above-mentioned expenditure cuts should probably be maintained even if growth turned out higher.

Structural reform

In the context of the preparation for membership of EEA and, subsequently, EU membership, a number of deregulation measures affecting the business sector have been implemented, as described in detail in Part IV. Concerning the public sector, as described in last year's *Survey*, the federal railway system, ÖBB, has already gone part of the way towards conformity with EU rules by splitting its operation into two independent agencies responsible for, respectively, the infra-structure and provision of services (*i.e.* running the trains). As regards the provision of services, pricing is no more under parliamentary responsibility (the relevant Article of the Federal Constitutional Law has been amended) but is the autonomous task of the enterprises. According to the Federal Railways Law of 1992, the Minister of Transport retains the right to issue specific orders concern-ing the running of the company in two cases only: the carrying through of the principles of transport policy in general; and *force majeure*.

With respect to the public sector proper, in addition to the above-noted public sector pay reform, aimed at rewarding job flexibility and management responsibilities, a major reform has been the introduction in 1994 of budget programmes aimed at enhancing medium-term fiscal planning procedures. These programmes will set out a four-year budget target, provide information on devel-opments of individual expenditure and revenue categories relative to target and contain suggestions for measures to achieve the stated targets. In addition to this reform, the labour market administration, which had formed part of the federal administration, was made an independent agency in 1994. In connection with the reform, peripheral activities will be moved to relevant government agencies to allow the new entity to concentrate on its core functions in labour-market policy.

In the field of *privatisation*, progress has been relatively limited since the previous *Economic Survey of Austria*. In the context of the continued privatisation efforts of the industrial holding company, ÖIAG, a 20 per cent plus 1 share of the remaining 70 per cent holdings in ÖMV, the oil and gas company, have been sold (in total a majority of the stock). In addition, discussions have been undertaken concerning the sale of a further 25 per cent, mainly to Länder-owned energy suppliers. The biggest success, however, has been the sale of 51 per cent of the stake held by ÖIAG (amounting to Sch 6.8 billion) in VA Technologies, a mechanical engineering firm. Moreover, the Federal Real Estate Company, which was established in 1992, has begun selling apartments to tenants. However, the privatisation of the federal Government's 50 per cent stake in the Creditanstalt-Bankverein, which was expected to take place in 1994, has been delayed due to pressures for an "Austrian solution", which led to the withdrawal of a leading foreign bidder.

Privatisation is expected to gather momentum in coming years, partly because of privatisations already in the pipeline, such as Creditanstalt-Bankverein, but also because privatisation receipts will be an essential element in the retirement of government debt, contributing towards compliance with Maastricht debt targets. Among the most likely candidates for privatisation over the coming legislative period are the State Tobacco Company, companies belonging to the ÖIAG group and the remaining federal shareholding in Bank Austria, which has already been put up for sale. In the latter case, however, the city of Vienna continues to hold about half of the share capital. More generally, the privatisation programme has remained focused on federal holdings whereas the large industrial holdings of the city of Vienna, as well as important holdings by the Länder in the housing and energy supply sectors, have aroused little attention. This may reflect the fact that privatisation is primarily seen in Austria as a way for the government to raise revenue rather than as a means of improving efficiency.

III. Mobilising labour resources

Austria has traditionally been more successful than most OECD countries in avoiding major macroeconomic disequilibria. In particular, its inflation perform-ance has been relatively good, while the unemployment rate has consistently been below the EU average. However, this apparently favourable picture needs to be qualified. More recently, inflation has failed to decline to the same degree as elsewhere and the Secretariat's short-term projection has wages beginning to accelerate before unemployment has fallen very far from recession-induced highs. In addition, the share of the working age population actually employed is not particularly high in Austria. This is mostly because participation rates are low, particularly in some specific segments of the population; but it is also worrying that open unemployment, while still comparatively low, shows the same tendency to persist at higher levels after each cycle as in other European countries. Against this background, the current chapter examines the need for structural adjustment in the labour market, first with respect to unemployment persistence and secondly as concerns the relatively low labour supply.

Avoiding ratcheting-up of unemployment

Unemployment persistence seems to be as prominent a feature of the Aus-trian labour market (Diagram 13) as of labour markets in many high-unemploy-ment countries:[28]

- in the 20 years following the 1973 conjunctural peak, the unemployment rate has fallen in only six years, never more than two years in a row and never by more than 0.4 percentage points;[29]
- following each downturn, wages seem to begin accelerating at a higher level of unemployment;
- the rate of unemployment associated with a ''normal'' vacancy rate has ratcheted up over time;

Diagram 13. **UNEMPLOYMENT PERSISTENCE**

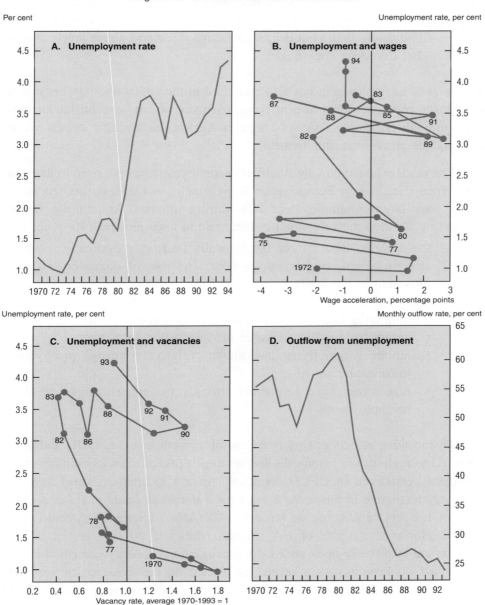

Source: OECD, Analytical Data Base and *Main Economic indicators* ; Pichelmann (1994).

- the rate of "outflow" from unemployment – *i.e.* the rate at which the unemployed either find jobs or leave the labour force – has fallen significantly in the last decade, although it remains above levels in most other European countries.[30]

The level of unemployment has also increased in the 1980s not only because of persistence phenomena but also of rising frictional unemployment: labour turn-over, through remaining relatively high in Austria, increasingly occurs via an intermediate phase of unemployment.

The main explanation why Austrian unemployment has not risen in line with experience elsewhere in Europe seems to be smaller increases during recessions rather than larger unemployment falls during upturns. Among the factors accounting for the relatively small cyclical rise in unemployment have been:[31]

- the Austrian labour force has typically been very cyclically sensitive, effectively buffering unemployment. The role of migration has been important in this context;
- employment has typically been more stable than elsewhere, reflecting the following factors, which again are interlinked:
  - output has been less volatile in Austria than elsewhere;
  - labour productivity has shown relatively strong pro-cyclical movements;
  - real wages have responded strongly to incipient signs of rising unemployment.

Disincentive effects arising from unemployment insurance (UI) and assistance (UA) regimes are among the factors most often cited as explaining unemployment persistence in OECD countries. Austria is often regarded as being relatively restrictive in this area, at least for a European country. It has a rather low pre-tax replacement rate as far as the UI (*Arbeitslosengeld*) system is concerned. However, the rate of UA (*Notstandshilfe*) is 90 per cent of UI and benefits are effectively open ended. Moreover, social security contributions are not levied on benefits. As a result, and based on the evidence of summary indicators of net replacement rates for different family situations and different durations of unemployment, Austrian generosity levels seem to be at least comparable to those in most other EU countries (Diagram 14).

Diagram 14. **UNEMPLOYMENT BENEFIT REPLACEMENT RATES
NET OF TAX, 1991**[1]

Per cent

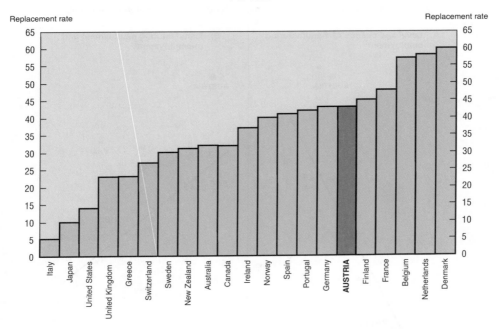

Replacement rate

1. The indicators of unemployment benefit generosity are calculated as a simple average of stylised replacement rates pertaining to persons at two different earnings levels, three different family situations and three different periods during an unemployment spell. The indicator is, thus, to be interpreted as a fixed-weight index of generosity, which does not take into account the actual distribution of the unemployed over these categories. The stylised replacement rates are based on detailed account of benefit entitlements. For further details, see OECD (1994*e*).

Source: OECD, *The OECD Jobs Study.*

Unemployment benefits may not only increase unemployment persistence but also the underlying level of unemployment. An example of such effects may be the extreme seasonal fluctuations in Austrian unemployment, which exceed those in most other countries, including countries where climatic conditions are at times difficult.[32] Indeed, implicit contracts between employers and employees in such sectors as tourism and construction may be tailored to take advantage of the UI system at times of seasonal slack, effectively leading to subsidisation of sectors with strong seasonal fluctuations in activity.[33]

Diagram 15. **MANUFACTURING EMPLOYMENT AND UNEMPLOYMENT**

Annual fall in manufacturing employment share, 1970-92,[3] percentage points

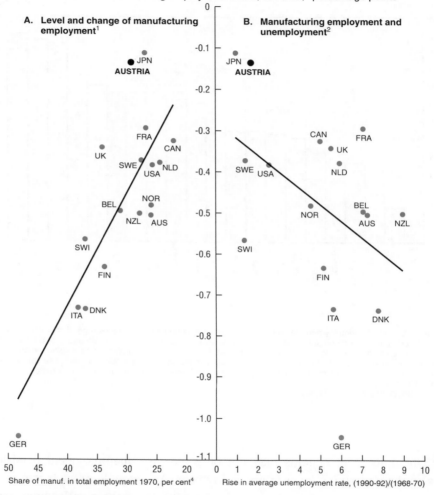

A. Level and change of manufacturing employment[1]

B. Manufacturing employment and unemployment[2]

Share of manuf. in total employment 1970, per cent[4]

Rise in average unemployment rate, (1990-92)/(1968-70)

1. The regression line corresponds to the estimated equation:
   <Employment change> = 0.36 − 0.03 * <1970 employment share>
           (2.12) (−5.02)   R squared = .63
2. The regression line corresponds to the estimated equation:
   <Rise in unemployment> = −0.28 − 0.04 * <employment change>
           (−2.36) (−1.89)   R squared = .19
3. Except for Netherlands (1975-1992).
4. Except for Netherlands (1975).
Source: OECD, *Labour Force Statistics.*

Tendencies for unemployment persistence could compromise the effects of structural reform and adjustment by generating upward pressures on unemployment. High unemployment in a number of other European countries may to some extent have been the consequence of labour shake-outs in the manufacturing sector combined with tendencies for unemployment persistence (Diagram 15).[34] So far, Austria has experienced only a modest reduction in manufacturing employment and currently has one of the largest manufacturing sectors, proportional to GDP, in the OECD area. But with pressures for structural adaptation rising, a necessary condition for avoiding a rise in structural unemployment may be rapid reallocation of labour across sectors. This may require a higher degree of relative (*i.e.* inter-sectoral and individual) wage flexibility, as well as a reduction in barriers to job creation in the service sector (see Part IV).

The institutional set-up of the Austrian wage bargaining system, interwoven with the chamber system (see Box 2), while making for *aggregate* wage flexibility, has also permitted a comparatively high degree of wage dispersion. Some

---

Box 2. **The Chamber system**

The institutional arrangements that form the framework of the social partnership are unique to the Austrian economy. On both sides of the labour market, there exists a parallel set of voluntary organisations (trades unions, industrial associations etc.) and self-governing bodies called chambers. Membership in the chambers is compulsory and the chambers are financed mainly through contributions related to the wage bill. The chambers on each side of the labour market are hierarchically organised with two central chambers for, respectively, workers and employers. In addition, farmers have a separate chamber.

The institutional centrepiece of social partnership is the so-called "paritetical" Commission for wage and price issues where, in addition to the central chambers, the Government and the Federation of Trade Unions are also represented. Four sub-committees are responsible for, respectively, the centralised surveillance of sectoral wage agreements, price developments and competition policy, wider issues of a social and economic character, and international issues.

Within this set-up, the chambers represent their members *vis-à-vis* the legislative and administrative powers. They have the right to present comments on government draft bills and, in addition, they are represented in many institutions. As a result, the social partners or, rather, their Chamber representatives, have a decisive influence on many aspects of policy. The Chamber system was described in greater detail in the *1989/90 OECD Economic Survey of Austria.*

Diagram 16. **RELATIVE WAGE DEVELOPMENTS IN SUBSECTORS OF INDUSTRY**[1]

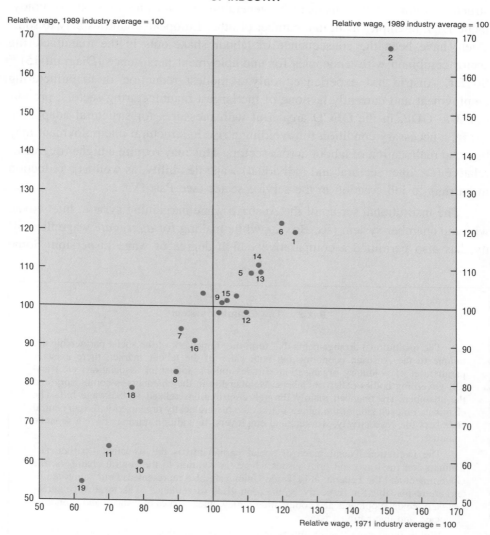

Relative wage, 1989 industry average = 100

Relative wage, 1989 industry average = 100

Relative wage, 1971 industry average = 100

Note: 1. Mining and iron works; 2. Petroleum industry; 3. Stone and ceramic industries; 4. Glass industry; 5. Chemicals industry; 6. Paper production industry; 7. Paper processing industry; 8. Wood working industry; 9. Food and beverage industry; 10. Leather production industry; 11. Leather processing industry; 12. Foundry industry; 13. Basic metals industry; 14. Machine tools industry; 15. Car industry; 16. Iron and metal goods industry; 17. Electrical industry; 18. Textile industry; 19. Clothing industry.
1. Based on average gross monthly earnings per employed.
Source: Butschek (1992); OECD.

changes are also observable in the relative wage structure over the past decades, though the basic patterns have remained relatively stable (Diagram 16). It is not clear to what extent this can be interpreted as a sign of sufficient wage flexibility given underlying productivity trends. But in light of expected rapid change in the future, a major challenge would seem to be the adjustment of labour market institutions so as to preserve high aggregate wage flexibility while seeking to enhance relative wage flexibility.

Making better use of potential labour resources

At 68 per cent of the working-age population in 1991, labour force participation is not much above the European average, and lower than in a number of comparable countries.[35] Indeed, since participation rates are usually higher where unemployment rates are lower, labour force participation seems surprisingly low. A cross-country estimation linking participation rates to unemployment rates for 1993 suggests that the Austrian participation rate is some 6 to 7 percentage points lower than could be expected based on the average cross-country pattern.[36] In international terms, the rate of employment is high for both young persons and prime-aged males, but employment rates are not particularly high for prime-age women and are low for older adults – a characteristic due not to particularly high unemployment but rather to comparatively low labour force participation (Table 12).

Among the most frequently cited causes of female labour-force non-participation have been lack of availability and relatively low levels of subsidisation of child-care facilities. However, enrolment rates for three to five year olds in pre-primary education, which includes nursery schools and kindergartens, do not appear to be particularly low in Austria.[37]

A more important cause of female non-participation may be an inadequate supply of part-time work.[38] Again, an assessment of this argument is not straight-forward. Certainly, the frequency of female part-time employment, at around 20 per cent of the total in 1992, is relatively low, but it is not *a priori* clear whether this is the result or the cause of the overall low labour-force participation.[39] However, general hindrances to competition, discussed in the subsequent chapter, may have retarded the development of the service sector, which in many countries provides a large share of part-time jobs.[40]

Table 12. **Non-employment rates for different population segments, 1991**

	Total working-age population	Prime-age		Young persons	Older persons
		Male	Female		
Austria	**34.2**	**8.2**	**37.5**	**30.8**	**76.0**
United States	29.5	14.8	30.0	45.0	47.0
Japan	26.4	4.0	36.3	57.0	35.0
Germany	34.1	7.8	30.2	28.0	62.0
France	39.7	10.3	33.7	69.0	65.0
Italy	39.9	10.6	52.6	69.0	67.0
United Kingdom	31.0	12.5	31.7	34.0	44.0
Canada	32.2	16.1	31.0	44.0	55.0
Australia	33.1	12.4	37.7	40.0	68.0
Belgium	42.8	11.2	43.1	69.0	78.0
Denmark	27.5	16.7	22.9	37.0	48.0
Finland	34.0	15.4	18.6	54.0	60.0
Ireland	48.3	20.2	61.5	63.0	62.0
Netherlands	37.1	9.5	44.4	44.0	72.0
New Zealand	34.6	19.6	35.0	48.0	58.0
Norway	27.2	12.2	23.3	49.0	39.0
Portugal	29.6	7.6	32.6	50.0	51.0
Spain	52.0	15.2	61.6	66.0	64.0
Sweden	18.4	6.1	9.5	39.0	24.0
Turkey	47.2	11.3	69.8	56.0	59.0
EU	38.1	10.9	40.4	51.6	60.9
OECD Europe	38.7	10.9	43.1	51.7	60.0
OECD	33.6	11.2	37.5	50.0	52.1

Note: The age groups are: prime-age: 25-54; young: 15-24; older 55+. In the cases of young and older workers, the area totals have been weighted together using total working-age population.
Source: OECD, *Labour Force Statistics.*

The low statutory retirement age of 60 for women evidently also tends to reduce their overall participation rates. Following a ruling by the Constitutional Court, the age of female retirement is to be raised to that of males (65 years), but since Austrian law prevents such changes from being applied retroactively, *i.e.* affecting persons already in the labour force, the rise in the female retirement age will only be phased in gradually, beginning in the year 2018.

In any case, the very low participation rates of older persons reflect strong incentives in the transfer system for taking early retirement. Indeed, only 8 per cent of men and 17 per cent of women remain in employment in the year prior to reaching the statutory retirement age. The average pension age for men has fallen from around 62 in 1970 to around 58 in 1992 (from around 60 to 57 for women).

Two schemes are mainly responsible for this development, between them covering 20 to 25 per cent of the population between 50 and 65 (Diagram 17):[41]

- The general early retirement scheme gives full pension entitlements for persons having worked 35 years and being 60 years or above (55 years for women). The net replacement rate under this scheme has been calculated at around 70 per cent.[42] In addition, early retirement can be obtained if an older person becomes unemployed, although in quantitative terms this scheme is less important.

- The number of disability pensioners has risen strongly and, at a total of around 400 000, it is now proportionately close to levels in the Netherlands, where high disability rates are considered a serious problem.[43] It is difficult to assess the stringency of Austrian administrative procedures in granting disability pensions. However, in 1992, of the total number of applications received, which have to be supported by medical advice, two-thirds were granted immediately. Of the rejected applications, roughly half of the applicants complained to the Social Court, which upheld their claim in about a third of cases.[44]

Diagram 17. **EARLY RETIREMENT AND INVALIDITY PENSIONERS**

Index, 1980 = 1

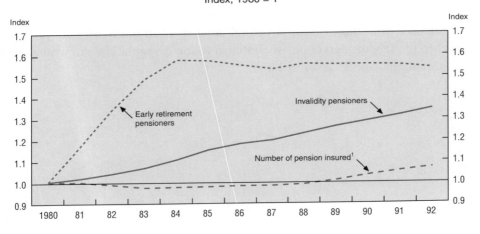

1. Total number of persons contributing to pension insurance.
Source: Handbuch der Österreichischen Sozialversicherung, various issues.

In the decade of the 1980s, net immigration contributed importantly to the growth of the labour force, foreign-born labour rising from 6.3 per cent of the labour force in 1980 to 9.0 per cent in 1991. Moreover, fluctuations in foreign labour effectively buffered employment and unemployment of Austrian-born labour. Indeed, the 1990-92 boom in employment, when it grew by 5.9 per cent, would hardly have been possible, or at least associated with much stronger inflationary developments, without the almost 4 percentage points contribution to labour force growth from foreign-born labour.[45] In this respect, the tighter migration regime introduced in 1993, with restrictions on both immigration and work permits for immigrants, implies that labour force cyclicality is likely to be less pronounced than previously.

Summing up

In conclusion, while it has been successful in maintaining relatively low unemployment, the Austrian labour market displays several of the characteristics making unemployment persistence and low participation potential problems. Among the factors responsible for unemployment persistence would seem to be elements of the transfer system. Among the factors making for a low participation rate, incentives to early retirement appear to be the key. Both sets of problems have implications for the strength and sustainability of the recovery and hence for the assessment of the current and prospective fiscal situation. Both also are associated with the case for structural adjustment in the future, not just with respect to the labour market *per se*, but also to the deregulation and institutional reform of the business sector at large.

IV. Challenges for the business sector

Introduction

The Austrian business sector has been characterised by a relatively good performance with regard to the macroeconomic fundamentals. Unemployment and inflation have been low and manufacturing productivity growth high. These strengths have, however, emerged in spite of structural weaknesses in sectors such as non-traded services, agriculture and the nationalised industries, where relatively high prices, inflation inertia and weak employment expansion betray the existence of structural rigidities. A process of rationalisation and subsequent privatisation, prompted in part by severe budgetary strains, has forced adaptation in the nationalised industries, and the latter process is still unfolding. Structural adjustment was accelerated by the establishment of the European Economic Area (EEA), which extended most of the provisions under the European Union's Single Market Programme to Austria prior to its accession. Thus, nearly all major remaining non-tariff barriers to merchandise trade had been removed (mainly by harmonising norms and standards), financial and most other services were liberalised, and free movement of labour established. Reinforced by membership of the EU and accentuated by developments in Eastern Europe, these reforms imply that competitive pressures are intensifying, posing new challenges for the business sector to adapt.

This Part first analyses the structural challenges facing the economy, particularly with respect to changing comparative advantage. The manufacturing sector will need to adjust toward higher technology activities in order to meet competition from Eastern Europe and indeed from other industrialising nations. Two of the essential ingredients in this process, the provision of finance and development of human capital, are discussed in the second section, together with the implications of the opening of the economy to the east. Remaining barriers to competition in the service sector need to be dismantled as the economy becomes integrated into the European internal market, and this process is discussed in the third section. The final section summarises the findings and discusses further policy initiatives which may be required on the part of the Austrian government.

Business sector performance

Output, employment, and prices: trends and structural features

The business sector – defined to include both private and public-owned enterprises, but excluding government services – accounts for over 80 per cent of Austria's gross national product, a proportion similar to that in other OECD Europe (Table 13). Within the business sector, the shares of manufacturing output and employment have been shrinking over time, to the advantage of market services – an OECD-wide phenomenon (Diagram 18). In Austria, however (as in Germany, Portugal and Spain), the shift into business services has been relatively slow. While employment in manufacturing declined substantially

Table 13. **International comparisons of business sector structure**

Per cent

	Share in 1991		Average growth 1980-91		
	Employees	GDP	Employees	GDP real	Deflator
Manufacturing sector					
Austria	35.3	31.0	–0.9	2.4	3.0
OECD Europe	36.1	24.9	–0.5	3.8	6.6
OECD	27.0	24.3	0.0	3.1	2.4
Market services					
Austria	61.6	62.0	1.3	2.8	4.5
OECD Europe	59.4	64.8	1.9	6.4	7.6
OECD	69.1	67.6	2.9	3.9	4.1
Business sector, as a per cent of GDP					
Austria	77.0	82.6	0.3	2.6	3.8
OECD Europe	73.6	84.3	0.8	5.6	7.1
OECD	81.9	88.2	1.9	3.6	3.5

Source: OECD, *National Accounts Statistics.*

Diagram 18. **SECTORAL EMPLOYMENT TRENDS**

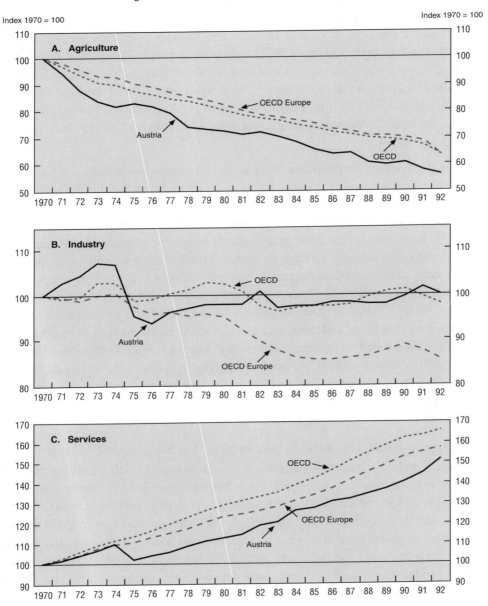

Source: OECD, *Labour Force Statistics*.

55

in the 1980s, the average annual growth of employment in market services was relatively weak (1⅓ per cent a year compared with 3 per cent in the rest of the OECD and 2 per cent in OECD Europe) and the rate of market service output growth was less than half the OECD European average. Partly as a result, the share of service sector employment of around 60 per cent, while comparable with the OECD Europe average, is significantly below the OECD average of about 70 per cent. Conversely, around 35 per cent of total business sector employment is still engaged in manufacturing compared with roughly 25 per cent for the OECD as a whole.

Manufacturing employment declines have been proportionally the largest in textiles and basic metals (3½ per cent annual-rate declines during 1980-92), both sectors being adversely affected by intensified world competition, especially from the non-OECD. While employment declines in textiles reflected shrinking output, those in basic metals reflected mainly sharp boosts in productivity (6 per cent annual rate). Productivity also grew rapidly in the heavily exposed paper industry (4 per cent annual rate), stimulated by an extraordinary 11 per cent average per annum growth in real gross fixed capital formation in this sector over the decade of the 1980s[46] (Table 14). At the other extreme, real fixed investment virtually stagnated in chemicals and there was a real decline in investment in basic metals – both nationalised industries undergoing extensive rationalisation after the mid-1980s. Among market services, employment gains were strongest in real estate, business services, miscellaneous social and personal services (2½ per cent annual rate increases) and tourism and financial services (2 per cent). Productivity increases were substantial only in transport and communications.

Austria's long-run inflation performance has been superior to the OECD average,[47] but the situation has recently been reversed, mainly reflecting high service price inflation. Since 1980, there has been particularly strong growth in the deflators for real estate, financial services, personal services, restaurants and hotels, and construction (Table 14). While rather large increases in the deflators were also registered for the open sectors chemicals and machinery and equipment, these are more likely to have reflected a reorientation toward higher value-added products as a way of coping with international competition.[48] Price *levels*, at the same time, are observed to be often much higher than OECD averages in both goods and service sectors. The greatest differentials (20 to 45 per cent) are to be seen in the prices of books and other printed matter, clothing and footwear,

Table 14. **The structure of the Austrian business sector**

Per cent

	Share in 1992		Average growth 1980-92			
	Employees	GDP	Employees	GDP real	Deflator	Investment [1]
Agriculture	1.2	2.9	−2.6	0.5	1.0	3.7
Mining	0.3	0.3	−5.7	−2.7	1.9	−3.3
Electricity, gas and water	1.6	3.3	0.0	2.5	2.8	2.6
Manufacturing	34.3	30.3	−1.0	2.2	3.0	6.7
of which:						
Food, beverages and tobacco	4.1	4.1	−1.1	2.6	1.5	5.2
Textiles, apparel and leather	3.2	1.7	−3.6	−1.0	3.2	6.1
Wood and wood products	3.9	2.2	0.0	2.6	2.4	7.4
Paper and paper products	2.6	2.2	0.0	4.0	1.9	14.7
Chemicals	3.0	4.5	−1.1	1.3	4.3	4.9
Non-metallic mineral products	1.9	1.8	−0.1	2.3	3.1	7.2
Basic metals	2.0	1.5	−3.3	2.6	−1.0	2.1
Machinery and equipment	13.7	12.3	−0.3	2.6	4.1	6.9
Market services	62.6	63.3	1.3	2.8	4.6	..
of which:						
Construction	10.4	9.0	−0.3	0.8	4.7	4.8
Wholesale trade and retail	18.8	15.7	1.4	3.0	3.1	..
Restaurants and hotels	6.0	4.3	2.1	1.5	5.6	..
Transport, storage and communication	10.3	7.8	0.9	4.0	3.0	..
Financial institutions and insurance	4.9	6.4	2.0	4.0	4.1	..
Real estate and business services	5.6	13.0	2.5	3.1	7.7	..
Community, social and personal services	6.6	5.2	2.6	3.6	4.9	..
Total business sector	100.0	100.0	0.3	2.5	3.9	5.2

1. Nominal, average growth 1980-90.
Source: OECD, *National Accounts Statistics.*

power, transport equipment and operation, communications, and recreational equipment and repairs (Diagram 19). Even *vis-à-vis* the EU, price differences for most products lie in the range of +5 to +40 per cent (communications) (Diagram 20). Such results suggest not only successful price discrimination between home and foreign markets in traded goods, reflected in large and persistent price differences, but also the effects of sheltering of services from international trade, reflected in large and growing price differences.

Diagram 19. **RELATIVE PRICE LEVELS[1] BETWEEN AUSTRIA AND THE OECD**
1990

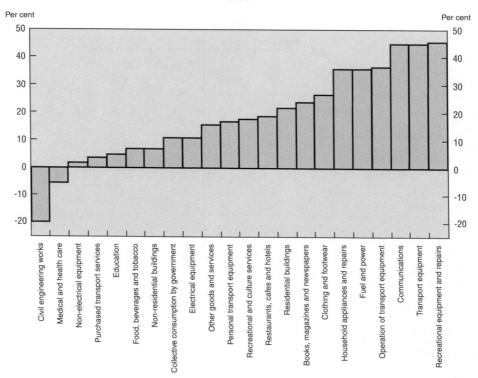

1. Defined as the percentage difference between the price level in Austria and the weighted average price level in OECD countries.
Source: OECD, *Purchasing Power Parities and Real Expenditures.*

International trade and comparative advantage

In contrast to their relatively small weight in output, market services play an unusually strong role in Austria's trade. Around 40 per cent of total goods and services exports are provided by market-service sectors, the highest ratio to be found within the OECD area (Table 15). This suggests a strong comparative advantage in services trade and a corresponding disadvantage in merchandise trade, the latter being reflected in a large and chronic trade deficit. As tourism

Diagram 20. **RELATIVE PRICE LEVELS[1] BETWEEN AUSTRIA AND THE EU**
1990

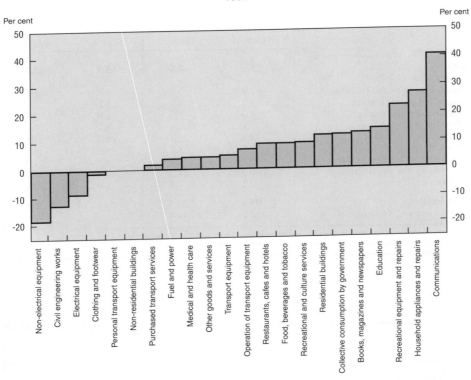

1. Defined as the percentage difference between the price level in Austria and the weighted average price level in EU countries.
Source: OECD, *Purchasing Power Parities and Real Expenditures.*

accounts for such a large share of service exports, however, there may also be an implicit comparative disadvantage in non-tourism market services and the recent and projected losses in the Austrian share of the tourism market point to the risks of overdependence on a single sector. These losses reflect *inter alia* structural factors tending to magnify the cyclical vulnerability of this sector, and to dampen the demand for Austrian tourism services in the longer run (Box 3).

Table 15. **Trade in manufactures and market services**

Per cent of total in 1992

	Austria		OECD	
	Exports	Imports	Exports	Imports
Manufactures	**55.6**	**64.8**	**65.3**	**60.2**
of which shares:				
Food, beverages and tobacco	2.9	3.8	7.6	8.2
Paper and paper products	7.2	4.5	3.8	3.6
Wood and wood products	5.0	3.3	1.9	2.6
Textiles	8.8	10.6	6.1	10.0
Chemicals	13.6	16.7	16.9	17.1
Basic metals	7.5	5.1	5.2	5.3
Non-metallic mineral products	3.1	2.1	1.7	1.7
Machinery and equipment	49.2	51.8	54.6	48.4
Other	2.2	1.7	1.9	2.9
Market services [1]	**39.4**	**26.7**	**23.6**	**23.8**
of which share: Tourism	50.6	44.4		

1. Defined as total exports/imports of goods and services less goods and factor income.
Source: OECD Trade Statistics; Austrian National Bank *Monatsbericht*.

Within manufacturing, Austria shows a higher degree of specialisation than the OECD as a whole in production and export of labour-intensive goods and "differentiated" (specialised-supplier) goods, while exporting and producing only half the OECD average in "science-based" (high-tech) categories (Table 16). Taking import as well as export ratios into account there emerges a significant revealed comparative advantage in resource and labour-intensive goods, slight disadvantages in scale-intensive and differentiated goods, and a strong disadvantage in science-based goods. Austria's areas of revealed comparative advantage within OECD manufacturing trade thus appear to be those which are now subject to intense competitive pressures due to growing trade with the non-OECD.

Indeed, an examination of the main manufacturing product groups shows that Austria's traditional areas of specialisation have often tended to be those showing the weakest medium-run export performance. Diagram 21, Panels A and B show that during the 1980s Austria suffered sharp losses of market shares in areas of strong specialisation relative to other OECD countries, such as wood and wood products, non-metallic mineral products (cement, glass, clay) and

Box 3. Challenges for the tourism sector

The tourism sector accounts for more than 8 per cent of total national output and employment, making Austria the most "tourist-intensive" country in the OECD. Austria has a 5½ per cent share of OECD tourism receipts (against a 1 per cent GDP share). Nevertheless, market shares have been in decline since 1975.

Main structural problems

Apart from the temporarily adverse income effects arising in the latest recession, which affected mainly the more cyclically-sensitive summer tourism, some of the chief problems afflicting Austrian tourism have been as follows:

- *Adverse relative price trends*: since European currency realignments in autumn 1992, the schilling has appreciated, on a trade-weighted basis, by 4 per cent. On top of this, Austrian price levels and inflation rates, especially in services, are relatively high. Empirical estimates suggest that about three-quarters of recent market share losses may be traced to adverse relative price movements.
- *Seasonal and regional over-concentration:* owing to the highly seasonal and region-specific nature of Austrian tourism (*e.g.* Alpine skiing and hiking), 44 per cent of overnight stays occur in the three months of February, June, and August, and overnight stays are concentrated in the western provinces and certain parts of Carinthia. This imbalance appears to be greater than in France or Switzerland, creating alternating phases of heavily strained capacity during peak periods – with environmental repercussions and over-work by employees – and excess capacity during the off-season. Thus in 1993, average capacity utilisation in this sector was around 30 per cent, and average unemployment was 18½ per cent.
- *Dependence on German demand:* with two-thirds of foreign overnight stays accounted for by German tourists, overdependence on one country makes Austria overly vulnerable to demand shifts in that country. Moreover, the average German tourist spends around 20 per cent less per diem than does the non-German foreign tourist.
- *Changing tastes and greater ease of foreign travel:* surveys show that the emerging new tourist – in Austria and elsewhere – seeks greater "adventure" and "learning" experiences. Cheaper air fares and package tours have at the same time enabled tourists to seek such experiences in new destinations abroad.

A new orientation

Proposals have been put forward for a medium-term programme to revitalise and restructure the tourism sector. They are interdependently geared to a) achieving a greater dispersion in supply and a diversification of demand; and b) adapting to changing tastes, via greater innovation. The main lines of the emerging new orientation are as follows:

(continued on next page)

(continued)

   – *Quality improvements:* to reduce the burden on the environment, itself a major element of tourism advantage, the aim is to raise tourism unit values while minimising volume growth. Moreover, a determined policy of quality improvements could enable the tourism industry to strengthen its competitive position despite the given high cost level. This entails focusing new investments on 3 to 5 star hotels, as well as upgrading restaurant and other tourism support services.

   – *Diversification of demand:* the goal is to increase the market share in dynamic regions such as the far east, via intensified marketing efforts and improved language skills among tourist employees.

   – *Reducing seasonal and regional concentration:* this involves moving to year-round tourism such as exists in France, Italy, and Switzerland, for example by stimulating more winter city-tourism and developing more conference, educational, and cultural tourism, as well as increased efforts in staggering holidays. The extension of store opening hours would also enhance the global attractiveness of Austrian tourism.

   – *Improving the human capital base:* this is a critical element of raising quality. Currently, there is a handicap in human capital formation oriented to this sector, especially at the management level. However, new Fachhochschulen are being established to deal with this problem.

Table 16. **Factor intensities in manufacturing production and trade**[1]

Per cent of total in 1992

	Output[2]		Exports		Imports		RCA index[3]
	Austria	OECD	Austria	OECD	Austria	OECD	Austria
Resource-intensive industries	30.6	34.7	15.8	15.7	12.6	18.3	1.46
Labour-intensive industries	21.0	16.1	18.4	12.5	19.4	17.2	1.30
Scale-intensive industries	32.5	31.8	31.9	32.4	32.2	29.7	0.91
Differentiated goods	12.1	9.5	26.9	24.0	23.8	20.5	0.96
Science-based industries	3.8	7.9	7.0	15.3	12.0	14.3	0.54
Total	100.0	100.0	100.0	100.0	100.0	100.0	–

1. See Annex III for classification of manufacturing industries.
2. In 1990.
3. RCA = revealed comparative advantage, defined as ratio of exports to imports for Austria, divided by the ratio of exports to imports of the OECD as a whole, for each category.
Source: OECD, *Foreign Trade by Commodities.*

Diagram 21. **EXPORT MARKET SHARES OF SELECTED MANUFACTURES**[1]

Index 1980 = 100

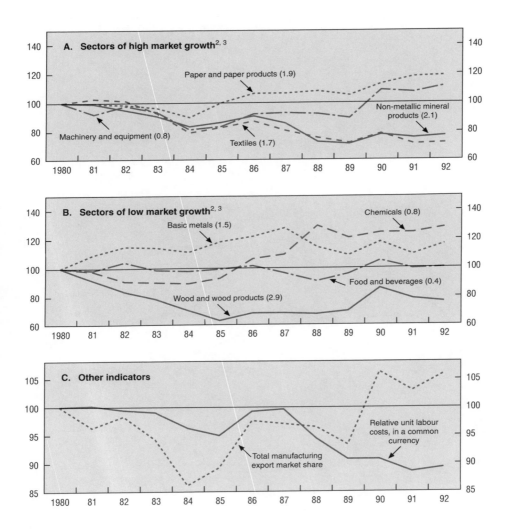

A. Sectors of high market growth[2,3]

Paper and paper products (1.9)

Non-metallic mineral products (2.1)

Machinery and equipment (0.8)

Textiles (1.7)

B. Sectors of low market growth[2,3]

Chemicals (0.8)

Basic metals (1.5)

Food and beverages (0.4)

Wood and wood products (2.9)

C. Other indicators

Relative unit labour costs, in a common currency

Total manufacturing export market share

1. Current prices.
2. High/low market growth sectors are defined as those where average sectoral market growth was higher/lower than average market growth in total trade during 1980-92.
3. Figure in brackets indicates 1980-92 average share in Austrian exports relative to share in total OECD exports.
Source: OECD, *Foreign Trade Statistics.*

Diagram 22. **EXPORT SPECIALISATION IN MANUFACTURING**
Share of Austrian exports relative to share of OECD exports

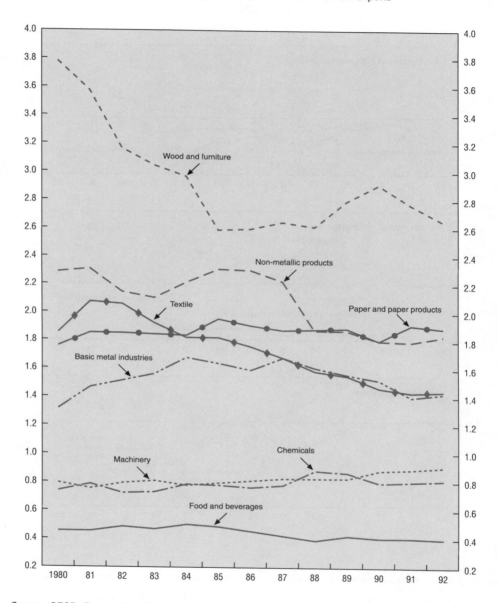

Source: OECD, *Foreign Trade Statistics.*

textiles (Diagram 22). Being not only resource and labour intensive, but also "environment" intensive, these products became less competitive *vis-à-vis* new competitors arising in the far east and, after 1988, in Eastern Europe – where the costs of resources, labour, and environment are lower. The only areas of specialisation showing strong export performance were paper and basic metals: both areas of strong productivity growth. Conversely, areas of relatively low specialisation have tended to show good performance. Chemicals and machinery and equipment, for example, picked up strongly after 1988 due to strong demand from Eastern Europe.

The overall pattern which emerges is one of Austria beginning to exploit new opportunities in markets of fast-growing demand, while boosting productivity in those sectors which have most effectively coped with new international competitive pressures. As a corollary of these trends, Austria's pattern of comparative advantage seems to be shifting in the face of export competition from the far east and Eastern Europe, whose areas of comparative advantage closely coincide with Austria's own traditional areas of export specialisation. As trade has opened up to the non-OECD – a trend, insofar as Eastern Europe is concerned, affecting Austria disproportionately because of its geographic location – the pattern of specialisation that had been appropriate to intra-OECD trade is adjusting towards those areas within which it had hitherto been weak and where capacity is underdeveloped: *i.e.* toward higher-technology manufactures, and value-added services. Austria's strong natural advantage in tourism has, up to now, afforded it some protection from such problems. However over-dependence on a single product group leaves the country exposed to output, employment, and balance of payments risks, reinforcing the need for a movement of resources toward emerging new areas of comparative advantage.

Productivity growth and innovation

Austria's overall export market share has, by and large, risen since 1984, the tendency for effective exchange rate appreciation being more than offset by the benefits of relative wage moderation and strong productivity gains on Austrian unit labour costs (Diagram 21, Panel C). This productivity growth may have been partly cyclical but Table 17 shows that by 1990 output per worker in the business sector had risen to just below the OECD average, whereas it had been only two-thirds the OECD average in 1966. This demonstrates a strong catch-up process,

Table 17. **Business sector productivity**

	Average annual growth rates, per cent						1990 productivity levels [1] (US = 100)
	Total factor productivity			Labour productivity			
	1974-79	1980-85	1986-93	1974-79	1980-85	1986-93	
Austria	**1.0**	**0.3**	**0.5**	**3.1**	**1.6**	**1.5**	**82.1**
Germany	1.7	0.4	1.0	3.0	1.3	1.6	86.7
France	1.6	1.0	1.4	2.9	2.2	2.2	97.7
Italy	1.9	0.6	1.3	2.8	1.3	2.1	74.2
United Kingdom	1.9	1.5	1.5	2.8	2.4	1.9	83.0
Belgium	1.3	1.3	0.9	2.7	2.5	1.7	91.8
Denmark	0.8	1.2	0.7	2.3	2.1	1.8	76.5
Finland	1.2	1.8	1.5	3.2	2.7	3.5	73.1
Ireland	1.6	2.0	3.3	3.4	4.2	3.9	73.4
Netherlands	1.6	1.0	1.1	2.6	1.9	1.2	93.3
Spain	0.3	1.8	1.0	3.2	3.7	2.2	71.1
Sweden	0.3	0.8	0.8	1.4	1.6	2.1	74.6
Switzerland	−0.5	0.2	0.5	0.8	0.6	1.6	82.3
OECD average	0.5	0.7	0.8	1.5	1.6	1.5	86.5

1. Based on 1990 purchasing power parities, business sector output per worker.
Source: Englander and Gurney (1994).

which occurred overwhelmingly in the open sectors: manufacturing productivity increases since 1974 have been much greater than in Germany, whereas productivity growth in the rest of the business sector was slightly slower – suggesting a relatively poor performance on the part of the service sectors (Diagram 23).

Reflecting the nature of the catch-up process, a significant part of the early productivity increases (one-half prior to 1973), arose from total factor productivity (TFP) growth (technological progress and other intangible elements). In the more recent period, as the productivity gap narrowed, TFP's contribution declined (to about one-third), while TFP growth itself slowed sharply in the 1980s and early 1990s. While a slowing also occurred in other European countries, it was from much higher rates of total factor productivity growth in the late 1970s. Indeed, during the 1980s Austria's rate of TFP growth fell to among the lowest in Europe and well below the OECD average.[49] The fact that Austria's labour productivity growth remained at the OECD average was due to continuing

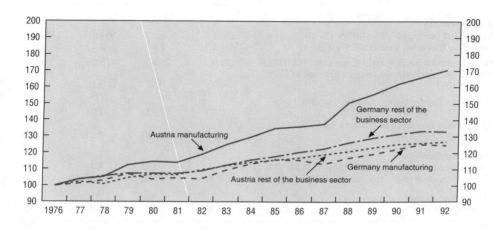

Diagram 23. **LABOUR PRODUCTIVITY IN AUSTRIA AND GERMANY**[1]
Index 1976 = 100

1. Real production per employee.
Source: OECD, *National Accounts*.

strong capital-for-labour substitution, a feature related to the above-average investment share in GDP.[50]

Empirical work suggests that the relationship between productivity growth and domestic innovative activity has become much stronger in Austria than in the past, with the estimated rate of return to industrial R&D having risen from very low levels in the 1970s to 30 to 40 per cent in the 1980s.[51] Such a relationship would suggest that the slowing of TFP growth since 1979 is due to an inadequate matching of Austrian innovation and R&D to the productivity level that by then had been achieved. In other words, as productivity levels came nearer to those prevailing abroad, Austria could no longer count simply on "osmosis" effects from abroad to ensure a fast pace of technological progress, but had to participate with an innovation effort of its own.[52] Comparison of various indicators of innovative activity with other European countries at similar (high) productivity levels tends to give *prima facie* support to a relatively weak innovative effort (Table 18). Per capita spending on R&D is only half that in Switzerland and

Table 18. **Innovative activity**

	Austria	Switzerland	Germany	Netherlands
R&D spending				
Total R&D per capita US$ at PPPs (1990)	236.4	575.9	504.9	322.8
Total R&D, as a per cent of GDP (1990)	1.5	2.9	2.7	1.9
Growth of total R&D spending, per cent, 1981/1991	28.0	25.0	15.0	9.0
Growth of total R&D spending as per cent of GDP, 1981/1991	0.33	0.57	0.36	0.17
R&D spending by business sector, per cent of GDP (1989)	0.80	2.14	2.07	1.26
Government assistance to business R&D, per cent of GDP (1989)	0.045	0.017	0.228	0.134
Patent applications				
Resident patent applications/10 000 population (1991)	2.7	4.6	4.1	1.1
External/resident patent applications (1991)	4.48	8.87	4.64	11.12
Technology balance of payments [1]				
Coverage ratio (1990)	0.32	..	0.83	0.53

1. Balance of international sales and purchases of intellectual property (patents, licenses, processes, know-how, design) and of international trade in services with a high intellectual property content (engineering studies, technical assistance, R&D services).
Source: Beirat für Wirtschafts- und Sozialfragen (1994); OECD, *Main Science and Technology Indicators.*

Germany and two-thirds that of the Netherlands; government support of business R&D (as a per cent of GDP), while smaller in Switzerland, is five times higher in Germany and three times higher in the Netherlands. Resident patent applications per capita are significantly fewer than in Germany and Switzerland, though more numerous than in the Netherlands. And the export-to-import ratio of intellectual property or services with a high intellectual property content remains relatively low. These findings are consistent with the above-noted comparative disadvantage in science-based trade and the very low proportion of science-based output.

Relatively low R&D investment might be related to the large presence of multinational firms (below), who typically undertake R&D in their home countries. However, a recent survey of innovation in industry cites a shortage of capital as the principal hindrance to innovative activity in Austria, especially among smaller firms.[53] Other factors involved are the small pay-off to innovation due to small home market size and uncertainty about market growth; organisational problems; regulations; and difficulty in obtaining personnel with the requisite R&D and production skills. Though factors such as lack of co-operation between research institutions and firms were cited less often, anecdotal evidence suggests that deficiencies in R&D co-ordination may also be important. Apart from the relatively low level of government aid to R&D, the perceived lack of certain types of capital suggests possible distortions in financial markets. Insufficient availability of people with advanced skills suggests problems in education and training. The problems of excessive regulation and small home market size may be mitigated by EU membership, which may also give scope for achieving more rapid productivity growth in the service sectors through removal of barriers to entry and operation there (see below). But, Austrian firms would need to step up their own innovative efforts in order to be able to reap benefits from EU research programmes.

The role of firm size and ownership structures

The contribution of large-scale enterprises to industrial (including craft) employment is small in Austria: only 26 per cent of employment is accounted for by firms with more than 500 employees. Nevertheless, average firm size is higher than the EU at large because there are also proportionately fewer small enterprises (in the one to twenty employee range) (Table 19). In the market-service sector, where the average firm size is only one-third that in industry, firm size as measured by concentration ratios is also predominantly small-to-medium, except where there are state-controlled monopolies as in telecommunications and rail transport (see Annex Table A1). The relative advantages or disadvantages of such a size distribution have been the subject of much debate, with small and medium-sized enterprises (SMEs) often associated with the following characteristics :[54]

- SMEs are generally more *profitable*, reflecting higher rates of return and possibly higher risk;
- large firms benefit from reduced per unit costs and lower risk via *economies of scope* (product diversification) and *scale* (spreading of fixed costs and trade-based market diversification), implying possible efficiency gains as firms grow.

In Austria, profitability is indeed, on the whole, inversely related to firm size, particularly in non-manufacturing, while efficiency rises with firm size especially

Table 19. **Distribution of industrial enterprises and employment by enterprise size**[1]

Percentages in 1991

	Enterprise size (number of persons employed)			
	0-19	20-99	100-499	500+
Distribution by number of establishments				
Austria	85.0	11.6	2.9	0.5
EU 12	93.3	5.5	1.0	0.2
Distribution by employment				
Austria[2]	22.1	24.3	27.7	26.0
Belgium	18.5	23.6	23.6	34.3
Denmark	30.6	23.8	22.6	22.9
France[2]	24.0	21.4	19.2	35.3
Germany[2]	17.2	17.8	19.7	45.3
Italy[3]	40.6	21.7	16.7	21.1
Norway[2]	27.3	22.7	23.2	26.8
Portugal	23.5	29.9	26.5	20.1
Spain	43.7	23.2	14.9	18.1
Switzerland	23.5	27.3	27.0	22.2
United Kingdom	26.5	13.1	15.0	45.4
EU 12[2]	28.2	19.7	18.1	34.0

	Austria	EU 12
Memorandum items:	Average enterprise size (1988)	
Industry	22	17
Services	7	5
Overall	11	7

1. Manufacturing, energy and construction.
2. 1990.
3. 1989.
Source: European Commission (1994).

in manufacturing (Table 20). This suggests, first, that the above-noted inflation pressures and high-price biases in the service sector would tend to abate as that sector opened up and expanded. And second, larger manufacturing firm size would result in higher overall productivity, helping to raise the relatively slow rate of TFP growth. Indeed, economies of scale and scope in manufacturing seem to be largely unexploited: on an OECD-wide comparison, Austrian (like Italian) firms show below-average economies of scale and scope both in exports and production (Diagram 24).

The lower profitability of large firms in manufacturing, while reflecting the fact that they are in internationally less profitable sectors, could also reflect in part the fact that they are (or have been until recently) heavily state-owned or

Table 20. **Firm size and performance**

	Efficiency		Profitability	
	(Value added per worker; total manufacturing = 1.00)		$\% \left[\dfrac{\text{Value added minus wages}}{\text{Value added}} \right]$	
	Manufacturing	Non-manufacturing	Manufacturing	Non-manufacturing
0 to 99	0.75	0.82	34.0	41.8
100 to 499	1.02	0.96	26.6	37.4
500 to 999	1.11	0.92	27.8	29.5
1 000 and more	1.35	0.99	30.7	27.9
Total	1.00	0.87	30.5	36.6

Source: F. Schneider (1991).

owned by state-owned banks (Annex Table A2). Empirical work has given evidence of labour cost inefficiency, low profitability, and low productivity in the state-owned industries.[55] However, the scale of publicly-owned manufacturing firms has been significantly reduced in recent years. Moreover in firms which are still nationalised (there are plans to privatise all of them), market-oriented ration-alisation and planning measures have been introduced, which is more likely to assure business-like behaviour on the part of managers. All this has resulted in a strong turnaround for the still-nationalised sector by 1994, such that a number of these firms are now ready for privatisation, which in turn could significantly improve the profitability and efficiency profile of larger firms. Furthermore, unlike in many other European countries, direct state aid to the private business sector appears to be relatively low, which could help to limit the distortions to resource allocation and comparative advantage that is implied by state participa-tion and intervention in business sector activity (Table 21).

Foreign multinationals now own five of the top 20 industrial enterprises (Annex Table A2), and have a strong presence in the insurance industry and distribution. In all, foreign-controlled companies generate around 15 per cent of total employment. Most economic arguments would suggest that direct invest-ment inflows raise economic performance – through infusions of capital and know-how, and stimulation of economies of scale and scope through greater firm concentrations under foreign control. Moreover, since the opening of the east and

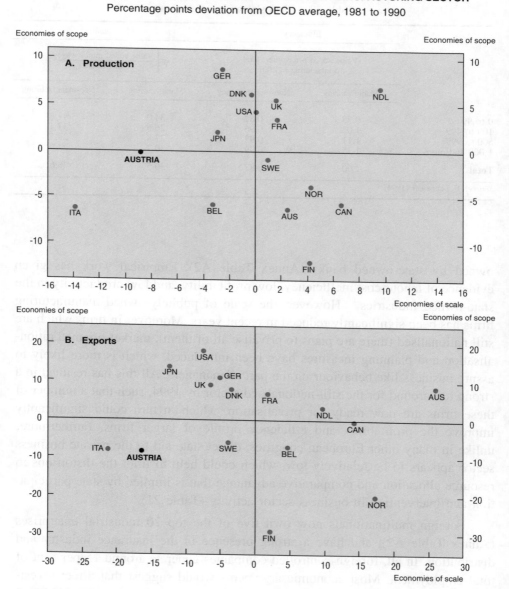

Diagram 24. **ECONOMIES OF SCALE AND SCOPE IN THE MANUFACTURING SECTOR**[1]

Percentage points deviation from OECD average, 1981 to 1990

1. Share of manufacturing industry subject to economies of scale and economies of scope, respectively. For classification of industries, see Annex III.

Source: OECD, The OECD STAN database for industrial analysis.

Table 21. **Government aid to the business sector**

	1986	1994[1]
By objective[2] (in per cent of total)		
R&D	9	24
Environment	7	14
SMEs	11	12
Tourism	13	11
Regional	3	4
Sectoral	7	35
General	50	–
Total	100	100
By instrument (billion schillings)		
Subsidies[3]	6.2	8.0
Federal government	5.1	5.8
Grants	–	4.8
Interest subsidies	–	1.0
Länder	1.1	2.2
Tax credits[4]	1.4	1.0[5]
Total	7.6	9.0
(as a per cent of GDP)	0.5	0.4

	1986-88	1988-90
Memorandum items:		
Government aid as a per cent of GDP[6]		
Germany	2.5	2.4
EU	2.2	2.0

1. Estimate of the Austrian authorities.
2. Cash grants of the federal government only; excludes ERP funds and nationalised industries.
3. Including ERP funds; excluding nationalised industries.
4. Mainly R&D and export support.
5. 1992 level.
6. The below EU data has a wider coverage (having different definitions for tax concessions, and including, *inter alia*, subsidies for railways) than does the EFTA data on which the above Austrian data is based. Thus, comparison is difficult.
Source: Submissions by Beirat für Wirtschafts- und Sozialfragen; Ministry of Finance; Federal Chamber of Labour; European Commission (1992a).

application for EU membership in 1989, Austrian direct investment outflows have rapidly outpaced inflows (Diagram 25). Both small-to-medium sized firms and the nationalised firms have greatly increased their foreign presence in recent years, suggesting that Austrian firms themselves are benefiting from growing internationalisation. Indeed, as of 1992, direct investment outflows, scaled to the size of the economy, exceeded the OECD average by 20 per cent; direct investment inflows at the same time just reached the OECD average.

Diagram 25. **RELATIVE GROSS DIRECT INVESTMENT**[1]
Ratio, OECD average = 1

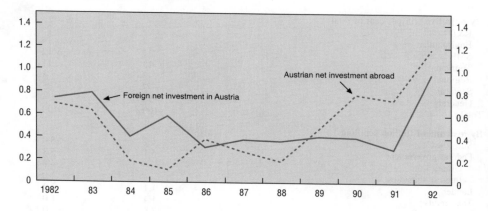

1. Austrian investment as a per cent of Austrian GDP relative to OECD investment as a per cent of OECD GDP, converted to dollars at daily average exchange rate.
Source: OECD, *International Direct Investment Statistics Yearbook, 1994.*

Meeting new competitive challenges

Broadening the capital market...

With its high overall savings ratio (in 1993, 25 per cent gross national savings rate compared with 19 per cent in the OECD as a whole), Austria would appear to be well positioned as far as capital availability is concerned. However (much as in Germany), household savings tend to be held in low-yielding bank savings deposit accounts. Corporate investments are consequently financed mainly by bank credits and own capital). While such a system may lower the cost of capital where banks are involved in enterprise monitoring and control, the absence either of market discipline or of ongoing bank monitoring could entail inefficiencies in financial resource allocation, due to an inability to price risk efficiently. The cost of capital, though benefiting from recent tax reforms, could thus be higher for certain types of investment than it would be if a broader capital market were available.

Despite rapid growth in recent years, stock market capitalisation, market trading volumes, and the popularity of owning shares remain low in international terms (Diagram 26). Trading is dominated by bank and insurance company shares, which account for 42 per cent of the total (Annex Table A3). With the energy and construction industries accounting for another 33 per cent, trading of shares of manufacturing and most market-service companies is insignificant, except for a few large, partly or formerly-nationalised companies. The securities (bond) market is about four times larger in terms of trading volume than the equities market. However, about 42 per cent of the outstanding bonds are issued by the public authorities, mainly the federal government, while over 50 per cent are issued by financial institutions, including mortgage bonds, municipal bonds, and cash bonds. With foreign bond issues accounting for 2 per cent of the market, corporate bonds account for less than 6 per cent, which is very low in international terms; by contrast, in the United States, almost 20 per cent of outstanding bond issues are those of non-financial corporations.

Business surveys cite a lack of access to capital as the number one impediment to greater innovative activity in Austria (above). In this context, business sector dynamism, as measured by entry and exit rates, may be impaired by the lack of vehicles for financing, buying and selling-off of firms. Rates of enterprise creation and destruction are in fact modest (Table 22). Weaknesses in the financial system may, on the one hand, inhibit the merging of companies into more scale-efficient or scope-diversifying units, and, on the other, block the formation of new, job-creating small firms, explaining the relatively low shares of firms in both the smallest and largest categories noted above. Moreover, for small new firms entering risky undertakings, particularly in the high-tech area, venture capital or start-up finance may be more relevant than capital market finance (which becomes realistic only after the firm becomes well enough established to go public). In Austria, however, there appear to be no special mechanisms in place for venture capital finance.

The underlying causes of inadequately developed capital markets and lack of venture capital finance are diverse, but include both disclosure requirements, which could increase liability to taxation, and the high issuance costs of shares. The supply of equity capital is also reduced by a traditional avoidance by the population of ''speculative'' savings instruments, a past history of insider trading, which increases perceived capital market risk, and market inefficiency due to

Diagram 26. **RELATIVE IMPORTANCE OF THE EQUITY MARKET**

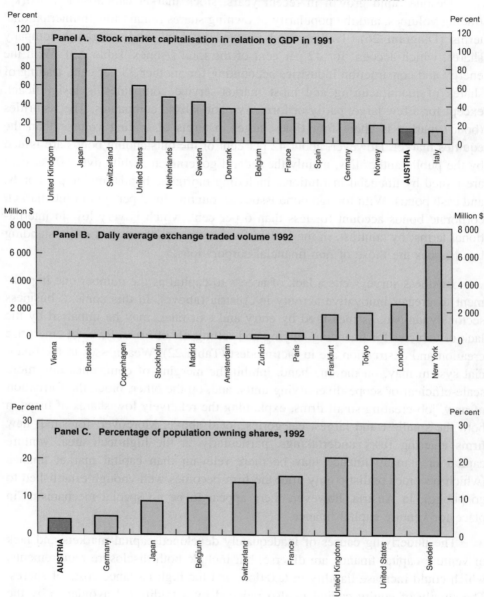

Panel A. Stock market capitalisation in relation to GDP in 1991

Panel B. Daily average exchange traded volume 1992

Panel C. Percentage of population owning shares, 1992

Source: The Austrian National Bank.

Table 22. **Entry and exit rates of firms**

Period averages

	Period covered	Establishment entry rates [1]	Establishment exit rates [2]
Austria	**1984-92**	**8.9**	**7.9**
Canada	1984-91	19.1	16.3
Sweden	1987-92	16.8	14.6
Denmark	1984-89	14.2	13.6
France	1984-92	14.3	13.2
New Zealand	1987-92	13.7	14.5
Finland	1986-91	11.2	9.8
Italy	1984-92	11.8	9.9
United Kingdom	1987-91	9.2	8.5
United States	1984-91	13.6	9.2

1. New establishments during the year as a per cent of the total number of establishments present at the beginning of the year.
2. Closing establishments during the year as a per cent of the total number of establishments present at the beginning of the year.

Source: OECD (1994c); submission by Austrian authorities.

insufficient computerisation. In addition, Austria has no pension funds of any major significance which could help develop capital markets, the government-run, non-funded old-age pension scheme having impeded the development of private-sector, funded alternatives. At the same time, placement rules for other institutional investors, such as investment companies, are relatively restrictive. Smaller firms may face particular obstacles in tapping the capital markets, as still-low liquidity on these markets both raises per unit transactions costs and favours the issue of relatively large amounts.

The government has begun to address such problems. The *Kapitalmarktgesetz* (Capital Market Act) of 1992 provided a new legal basis for bond issues, whereby stringent disclosure standards for new issues replaced the formerly complicated procedure of Ministry of Finance approval. In 1993, a 22 per cent withholding tax on interest income was introduced, to be levied as a final tax. This replaced the former (higher) income and inheritance taxes on such incomes, and was combined with a tax amnesty for past non-payment of tax. To help stimulate the development of the equity market, the 1993 Amendment to the *Börsegesetz* (Stock Exchange Act) made insider trading a criminal offence. The creation of an independent market supervisory authority has been agreed to in principle.[56] Technical improvements are also being made to the stock market: an on-line share-analysis database system has been installed, screen-based stock exchange trading is planned as of 1995, and market trading has been extended by one hour. The 1994 tax reform also contained measures to improve the attractiveness of equity-market finance: the stock exchange turnover tax on securities lending and interbank trading was abolished, as was the wealth tax, which dissuaded many medium-sized family businesses from going public; and taxation of dividend income was brought into line with fixed-interest income, being made subject to the reduced 22 per cent income tax. Finally, the *Rechnungslegungsgesetz* (Accounting Act) has enforced greater transparency and clearer presentation of company balance sheets.[57]

...and enhancing the universal banking system

The obverse of underutilised capital markets is that banks play a preponderant role in the provision of outside finance to the business sector. This is largely consistent with the universal banking model, as found also in Germany and Switzerland. However, the Austrian model may lack some of the beneficial features found in these other countries, where close co-operation between banks and firms in the form of information sharing lowers the cost of credit, due to lower transactions and information costs, and also facilitates long-range planning, by increasing the lender's stake in keeping the company afloat and encouraging its active involvement in the future development of the company.[58] In Austria, by contrast, banks are apparently less directly involved in long-range planning and information sharing with firms. This could reflect the legacy of a large state enterprise sector, where banks faced low lending risks due to the "soft" budget constraints on the firms they lent to (or else the banks themselves were state-owned). In this climate, the development of close bank-firm relationships was largely unnecessary.

The dominant position of bank finance may be reinforced by the system of interest rate subsidies, as they are tied to bank loans.[59] Because of the paperwork burden and other costs, banks prefer to deal with larger firms as this minimises the per unit costs of administration. In general, small and medium-sized firms find themselves facing higher costs of credit than larger firms – a factor which may help to explain both their higher rates of return before financing costs and their failure to expand. Recent banking reforms and growing bank concentration in connection with the European internal market (below) may over time improve the bank allocation of credit to the business sector. However, the system of credit subsidies to business may stand in the way. These have been significantly reduced in recent years, but this process should continue in order to improve the functioning of capital markets and the allocation of resources.[60]

Developing human capital

Besides raising worker skills, human capital development is the key to R&D, innovation, and total factor productivity growth. By one key measure, rates of completion of secondary education (as the highest level of attainment), Austria scores very well with a 60 per cent rate, one of the highest in the OECD. This figure includes vocational education and training programmes in full-time schools and in apprenticeship, which cover over three-quarters of the secondary school population. However, in 1991, the proportion of the Austrian population with university degrees was about 7 per cent, compared with higher rates in Germany (11 per cent) and the Czech Republic (10 per cent) and substantially higher rates still outside Europe (Diagram 27). The number of scientific and engineering graduates in the total labour force is proportionately even smaller: 2½ per thousand as compared with 6 in Germany and 4½ in the EU.[61] The low rate of post-secondary graduates in Austria in part reflects the fact that the advanced level vocational colleges (*höhere technische Lehranstalten, Handelesakademien, Tourismusschulen*), while formally belonging to the upper-secondary school system, provide qualifications for many posts taken up in other countries by academics.[62] In this respect, the main feature of vocational training in Austria is its diversity. But this emphasis on vocational education and training at the upper-secondary level (full-time schools or apprenticeship) as the main vehicle for human capital development may be increasingly at odds with the advanced educational needs of a technologically-sophisticated economy. Furthermore, the number of non-university, post-secondary education institutions that might allow for the possibility to build on top of vocational training, as in the case of the German *Fachhochschulen* (polytechnics) is limited. The government is attempting to address such problems in part with the planned building of more Fachhochschulen, which are to serve as the focal points of regional "clusters" that would bring together in an effective way the demanders and the suppliers of human capital.

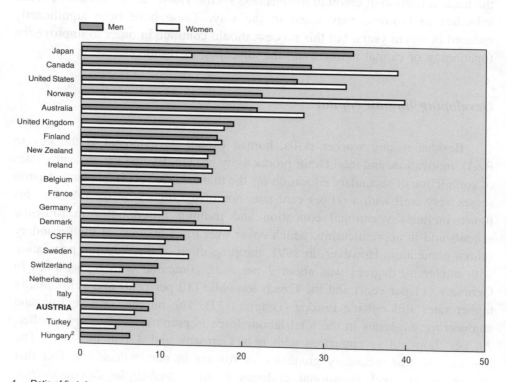

Diagram 27. **UNIVERSITY GRADUATION**[1]

Men   Women

Japan
Canada
United States
Norway
Australia
United Kingdom
Finland
New Zealand
Ireland
Belgium
France
Germany
Denmark
CSFR
Sweden
Switzerland
Netherlands
Italy
AUSTRIA
Turkey
Hungary[2]

0   10   20   30   40   50

1. Ratio of first-degree graduates from public and private universities to 100 persons in the population at the theorical age of graduation, men and women (1991).
2. Men and women.
Source: OECD, *Education at a glance, 1993.*

Opening the economy to the east

Recent trends

Correcting the deficiencies in capital-market finance and human capital development are the more critical because of the challenge posed by eastern European economies. Owing to its geography and history, Austria is likely to be disproportionately affected by the reform and opening of Eastern Europe. The importance of trade with its three Eastern neighbours – Hungary and former

Czechoslovakia and Yugoslavia – had been nearly equal to that of its three western neighbours in the late 1920s (Annex Table A4). Austria now has the opportunity to restore some of these historical linkages. This will lead to bigger export markets and new investment opportunities. The obverse is that Austria will now come under even greater pressure to adapt both in areas of traditional comparative advantage and where it is structurally weak. Popular fears both of low-wage competition and of ''environmental'' dumping have led to imposition of trade barriers in affected areas and demands for more. Immigration controls have also been tightened. However, theory and most empirical estimates suggest a net positive economic impact of opening to the east.

Since the opening process began in 1988, Austria's exports to eastern European countries have grown at an average annual rate of 20 per cent in schilling terms, while imports from them have increased by 15 per cent per year (Diagram 28). Austria has thus marked up significantly increasing trade surpluses with these countries (from Sch 9½ to 13 billion), adding to its own economic expansion. Austria now supplies 11.6 per cent of all OECD exports to these

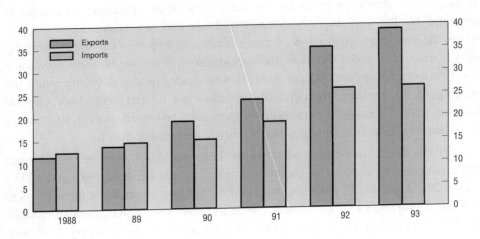

Diagram 28. **TRADE WITH CENTRAL AND EAST EUROPEAN NEIGHBOURS**[1]
Billions of schillings

1.   Hungary, the Czech Republic, Slovakia and Slovenia. Data for Slovenia begins in 1992.
Source: The Austrian National Bank.

Table 23. **The commodity composition of trade with Eastern Europe** [1]

Per cent

	Structure in 1992 (share of total)		Annual change in value 1989 to 1992	
	Exports	Imports	Exports	Imports
Food (0 + 1)	8.5	7.4	28.3	11.8
Raw materials (2 + 4)	2.4	13.1	13.1	1.7
Fuels (3)	2.1	28.7	61.3	3.1
Metal products (67 + 68 + 69)	12.0	11.1	–0.9	34.7
Chemicals (5)	12.6	6.2	13.2	3.8
Other semi-manufactures (6 – 67 – 68 – 69)	11.2	6.6	25.7	29.9
Machinery and equipment (7)	37.1	15.7	22.6	63.9
Textiles and apparel (84 + 85)	3.3	6.4	45.6	82.5
Other consumer goods (9 + 8 – 84 – 85)	10.7	4.7	42.4	43.1
Total	100.0	100.0	19.3	14.9

1. Commodity classification according to SITC (REV3).
Source: OECD, *Foreign Trade by Commodities.*

countries, and absorbs 7.3 per cent of all OECD imports from them; exports to Eastern Europe account for 11½ per cent of Austria's exports, and imports from these countries make up 7¼ per cent of the import total. The importance of classical trade flows, as predicted by the theory of comparative advantage, is suggested by the very high proportion of fuels and raw materials in imports versus the very high proportion of manufactures in exports (Table 23). Surprisingly, however, a more detailed decomposition shows that intra-industry trade now accounts for around 40 per cent of total trade, nearly doubling since the opening of the borders, though still far below its 63 per cent share of total Austrian trade.[63] Increased intra-industry trade may be traced, in turn, to growing cross-border production linkages due to direct investment flows.

Strong direct investment outflows to these markets helped to turn Austria into an overall net exporter of direct investment capital between 1989 and 1993[64] (Table 24). Austria's 11 per cent share of total foreign direct investment flows to in these countries is extremely large given its GDP weight. Austria also exhibits the highest number of participations in joint ventures in Hungary (although project size tends to be small). Austrian investments in these countries are found mainly in the retail, banking, and labour-intensive manufacturing sectors. In

Table 24. **Direct investment flows by region**

Schilling billion

	1980	1989	1990	1991	1992	1993	Direct investment position 1992[1]	of which: Nominal capital
Total inflows	**3.1**	**7.8**	**7.4**	**4.1**	**10.3**	**11.4**	**127.4**	**78.8**
of which from:								
Germany	1.1	3.0	3.3	3.2	4.1	3.0		23.0
Netherlands	0.4	3.6	−0.2	1.0	0.5	2.9		5.8
Other EU	−0.1	0.4	1.9	3.9	3.3	2.1		8.3
Switzerland	1.2	−0.5	0.1	−2.4	1.0	1.6		10.7
United States	0.3	0.1	0.3	−0.4	0.4	0.6		4.5
Total outflows	**1.3**	**11.4**	**18.5**	**15.0**	**20.6**	**17.1**	**86.5**	**45.3**
of which to:								
Germany	0.1	3.4	3.2	2.3	4.2	1.5		9.0
Netherlands	0.0	1.5	−0.2	0.8	0.1	0.3		1.9
United Kingdom	0.0	0.7	1.7	3.3	5.1	2.1		4.4
Italy	0.0	1.0	1.9	1.0	0.4	0.5		1.0
Other EU	0.6	0.2	0.7	3.8	2.2	2.2		..
Switzerland	0.1	1.1	3.1	−1.9	..	0.8		4.4
United States	0.2	1.5	1.4	0.9	0.5	1.6		3.7
Hungary	0.0	0.7	4.0	4.4	3.2	2.9		9.4
Other CEE	0.0	0.0	0.2	1.5	1.7	3.2		..

1. Regional breakdown for total equity not available.
Source: OECD, *International Direct Investment Statistics Yearbook*; and Austrian National Bank.

addition, Austria's strategic location has attracted a sizeable inflow of western companies' branch offices (some 1 000 thus far) using Vienna as their base to cover eastern markets. Austria is also developing the capacity to export communications and consulting services in conjunction with its growing role as "springboard" to the east.[65]

Structural changes and the gains from trade

As already noted, there are both winners and losers from trade with Eastern Europe. Downward pressures on prices and profits, and growing bankruptcies, are likely to result in sectors directly competing with imports from the east. These so-called "sensitive" sectors are often identified as mining and minerals, food products, steel, leather processing, clothing and textiles. In such sectors, output, investment, and employment will ultimately fall, and adjustment costs may be substantial because of the regional concentration of industries, sector-specific skills and capital stocks. Conversely, firms exporting to Eastern Europe may find sales and profits increasing due to a fast-growing new market as well as the competitive advantage over other supplier countries implied by closer direct-investment and historical-geographical relationships. Given the severe capital deficiency in Eastern countries, the most competitive Austrian exports are likely to be in the capital- and technology-intensive areas. In such sectors, output, investment, and employment will rise.

In many cases, the development of intra-industry trade, like inter-industry trade, is based on differing relative factor prices reflecting relative factor scarcities between Austria and the east: low labour costs coupled with a high-quality labour force in Eastern Europe induce the relocation of production facilities to these countries (Table 25).[66] Such relocations often imply cross-border production linkages, and hence often shipments of the same good in various stages of production, which are recorded as intra-industry trade. Although such trade is also likely to be associated with job losses in sectors whose comparative advantage has declined with the opening of Eastern Europe, such job-losers are more

Table 25. **Education and earnings in Austria and Central-Eastern Europe**

	CSFR[1]	Hungary	Poland	Austria	Germany
Gross monthly earnings in $US (1991)	135.8	213.5	161.6	2 003.3	2 797.4
of which: Manufacturing	..	186.9	151.4	2 276.7	2 239.8
Highest level of education, as per cent of labour force (1990)					
Compulsory education	26.0	38.4	34.2	28.8	25.6
Secondary school	64.8	50.0	57.4	64.1	60.0
Higher education[2]	9.2	11.6	8.4	7.1	11.0
Specialisation as per cent of higher-educated population (1989)					
Engineering	38.9	21.7	16.9	12.5	20.9
Natural sciences	2.6	4.2	2.9	8.5	7.1
Medicine	6.6	7.3	15.6	14.3	24.3
Education	17.8	35.3	29.5	14.4	7.1
Other	34.0	31.5	35.1	50.3	40.6

1. Former Czech and Slovak Federal Republic.
2. University and technical colleges.
Source: Mayerhofer (1992); OECD (1993a).

likely to find new employment than those in contracting sectors, as other firms in the same industry will be expanding; *i.e.*, the existence of the entire sector is not in jeopardy as in the case where inter-industry trade is shifting. On the contrary, the ability to profit from relative factor price differentials with Eastern Europe is likely to lead to substantial trade creation.

Mutual terms of trade gains result from the fact that, prior to trade, the relatively abundant factor in each country (in this context, capital in Austria, and labour in the east) displays a lower relative price than in the other country; thus, export of the products which use the relatively abundant factor intensively leads to higher export prices (increased demand) and lower import prices in each trading country.[67] Productivity gains would tend to arise from the more appropriate specialisation pattern, the pressure to strengthen comparative advantage (endogenous technological change), or from the reaping of greater economies of scale and scope through access to larger markets. Direct factor movements also lead to gains. Direct export of capital to the eastern European economies builds up their capital stocks and raises capital intensity and profitability, leading to more rapid productivity gains and higher levels of prosperity than if these countries had to finance capital accumulation only out of domestic saving. This in turn generates more rapid market growth for Austrian exports and may enhance political stability, thereby slowing immigration from these countries into Austria. Of course labour flows from these countries are also a consequence of relative factor price differences but the magnitude is now limited by immigration controls.

Empirical assessments of the prospective impact of the opening of the east on the Austrian economy have tended to focus on the labour market, but the estimates of the net job change, *i.e.* the balance between job destruction and job growth across the different sectors, vary from study to study.[68] What is undeniable is that certain sectors will face a heavy restructuring burden, and the net employment effect will be the more advantageous the more successful Austria is in meeting the restructuring challenge over the medium term. Indeed, a case could be made that existing empirical studies seriously underestimate the welfare benefits of east-opening. First, the beneficial impacts of growing intra-industry (co-operative) trade, discussed above, are difficult to model and these studies so far have focused exclusively on inter-industry (competitive) trade. Second, the income-generating effects of mutual terms of trade and productivity gains

– *i.e.* both domestically and abroad – tend to be ignored. Domestically, these will lead to higher spending in all sectors, including non-traded goods, and abroad to higher market growth for Austrian exports.

The sheltered sector and the impact of European integration

In adapting to the challenge from the east, and in correcting the deficiencies in capital market finance and human capital development, an important obstacle is the generally low level of product market competition in Austria, which impedes the structural flexibility of the business sector. As was discussed in the 1990 *Survey*, competition in the sheltered service sectors has been traditionally stifled by a web of regulations governing both market-entry and the operation of businesses. This resulted in higher prices for the consumer and rent-seeking behaviour by firms. Competition in industry, although far more developed than in services due to general trade openness, has been hampered by relatively high trade barriers against some Eastern Europe and East Asian countries (see 1993 *Survey*). This section provides a report on the progress towards a more competitive environment, focusing on the impact of the EEA and EU entry.

The process of integration with the European community is much more advanced than that with Eastern Europe, having started more than 30 years ago with the establishing of EFTA in 1960 and continued with the first EFTA-EC free trade agreements in 1973. As result, by 1980, 80 per cent of Austria's trade was with the European Community, and over 40 per cent with Germany alone. Moreover, 70 per cent of such trade was of the intra-industry type, reflecting similar economic structures and integration through trade and direct investment flows. Direct investment flows into Austria, especially from Germany, have been strong since the early 1970s; however, since 1989 (the year Austria made its formal application for EU membership), Austrian investments flows to the EU have exceeded those from the EU to Austria (Table 23 above). The integration process has now reached its final stages with the formation of the EEA as of 1 January 1994 and EU membership as of 1 January 1995 (Box 4).

The economic implications of participation in the EEA and of EU membership are quite distinct. The EEA embodied the "four freedoms": free flows of goods, services, capital, and labour. As freedom for goods and capital flows had already been largely accomplished, the major impacts are in services trade and

86

Box 4. **Integration effects of EEA participation and EU membership**

EEA PARTICIPATION	EU MEMBERSHIP
The "four freedoms":	**Internal market:**
Goods trade[1]	Customs union
Services trade[1]	Common agriculttural policy (CAP)
Capital flows	Common external trade policy
Labour movements[2]	Structural policy
	Regional policy
Competition law	Industrial policy
	Tax regimes (harmonisation
Other areas:	of indirect taxes)
Consumer and health protection	Participation in EC budget
Transportation (transit agreements)	(net contributor)
Research and information	
technology	**Maastricht agreement:**
Education	Economic and monetary union
Statistics	(EMU)
Business law	European union (EU)
	Common external and security
Partial harmonisation of:	policy (CESP)
Social policy	Co-operation in judicial
Environmental policy	and internal matters
Agriculture and fisheries	(EU-citizenship)

---

1. Limited integration, given continuation of border controls between EU and EFTA states. Implies disadvantage for EFTA states in trade with eastern Europe in partially processed goods.
2. Freedom of movement for workers and self-employed; right to establish branches.
Source: Breuss *et al.* (1994).

labour flows. The EFTA countries' service sectors were formally integrated into the internal market, and EU competition policy was adopted into their legal frameworks (Diagram 29). The main additional effects of EU membership – apart from the fact that trade is more fully liberalised in the context of a customs union and there is a common external trade policy – is that the process of integration is extended to agricultural, structural, regional, industrial, and tax policies within the context of the internal market. In the process, the liberalising of the service sector, begun under the EEA, will be intensified.

Diagram 29. **POLICY CONVERGENCE IN THE PROCESS OF EUROPEAN INTEGRATION**[1]

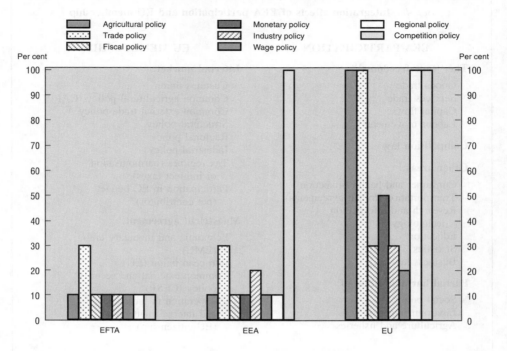

1. Qualitative indices, reflecting extent of policy harmonisation between Austria and the EU. 100% represents full harmonisation.
Source: WIFO, *Monatsberichte 1994*.

Progress in deregulation

Because of "natural" entry barriers such as high fixed costs and high product differentiation, the market structure in many services is intrinsically that of imperfect competition characterised by economies of scale and scope (Annex Table A1). In addition, government regulations, ostensibly put in place to correct for externalities have provided protection (whether intended or not) to many such sectors. In the EU and in Austria, intensified competition, arising from deregulation, is likely to increase concentration as firms seek to cut costs by pooling their resources and risks. To some extent this has already taken place in anticipation of the internal market. Between 1987 and 1991, direct foreign investment rose at an above-average rate in both EU and EFTA countries (*e.g.* in insurance) and "strategic" merger activity increased significantly in such areas as banking and air transport. However, apart from air transport, where fares have been reduced in the battle for market shares, the expected price and welfare effects of greater competition have been slow to materialise. This is, in part, because adjustment to the new environment has proved to be slow, and implementation of reforms is not yet complete; in addition, the trend toward greater firm concentration has blunted the impact of increased competition. Thus, in financial services, economies due to mergers and cross-border acquisitions have led to higher profits rather than lower prices to consumers.[69] In areas such as distribution, where the trend toward greater concentration involving foreign capital has also accelerated recently, significant price reductions have yet to be observed, while thus far the telecommunications sector has been slow to adjust in anticipation of new market conditions. Moreover, the benefits of EU-wide public procurement on prices in the construction sector will materialise only gradually.

An important question facing Austria is to what extent it can be more successful – than has been the generalised EU experience thus far – in achieving price reductions and consumer welfare gains through intensified competitive pressure, while also realising the currently high potential for economies of scale and scope. EU membership also has the potential to create employment in sectors where regulations currently impede expansion. The following discussion assesses the major institutional changes and economic benefits that are expected to result from EU membership in the areas of telecommunications, banking, insurance, road transport, construction, and distribution.[70]

Telecommunications

This sector exhibits the highest degree of concentration, being a regulated monopoly under state ownership and consisting of two companies, Post- und Telegraphenverwaltung (PTV) and (the very small) Radio Austria Communications. As in many other OECD countries, cross-subsidisation is important, with the surpluses generated by the telecommunications monopoly being used to help cover losses both within the telecom branch internally and in the postal branch. However, Austrian telecommunications display a higher level of restriction than most OECD economies, as it remains one of the few OECD countries where the telephone monopoly is part of the ministry and is not yet a legal entity (Annex

Table A5). While reforms of the 1980s allowed private access to value-added services,[71] telecommunications in some respects does not meet OECD standards: telephone density (telephones per capita) is lower only in Belgium, Ireland and the southern European countries, and waiting times for obtaining a telephone line are comparable only in Greece, Portugal, and Turkey. Reflecting low competition and budget financing needs (telephone charges are set by Parliament), telephone costs in 1994 were 27 per cent above the OECD average.[72] However, due to cost reductions effective on 1 January 1995, telephone costs in 1995 should be nearer the OECD average.

In preparation for the internal market, the Telecommunications Law 1993 has eased restrictions on the establishment of value added telecommunications services by making them franchise-free; also, Europe-wide competition is allowed in the market for telephone apparatuses. Basically, only the provision of infrastructure and voice telephony remain reserved for the PTV. Future reforms should result from the fact that EU guidelines envisage open access to the network (Open Network Provision), and market access to all providers of telecommunications services is to be liberalised on the basis of objective and transparent criteria. But, at the same time, the EU allows for state monopolies to be dismantled only step-wise and with caution. Thus, liberalisation arising from the internal market is expected to be a very slow process, giving rise to only partial privatisation. Greater competition is in fact more likely to be enforced by technological change.[73]

Banking

The banking sector is characterised by oligopolistic competition, the eight major banks accounting for just over 50 per cent of banking business. At the same time, Austria has more banking branches per capita than any other OECD country. In international terms, bank size (even of the largest bank) is small, while profitability is low and stagnant. State control in the banking sector has fallen markedly over the last ten years in the framework of the government's privatisation programme. Foreign ownership of banks is still modest, even though the internationalisation of the banking sector, through direct investment flows, has been in progress since 1980. Austrian banks, on the other hand, are highly present in Eastern Europe.

Reforms were recently instituted in the banking sector via the 1994 Banking Act (*Bankwesengesetz*), fulfilling Austria's obligations under the EEA agreement to incorporate EU banking guidelines and recommendations into its own legislative framework. The most important of these reforms are implementation of the two guidelines on banking law co-ordination and rules on capital adequacy, solvency, balance sheet accounting and the supervision of banks, as well as the guideline on money laundering (though savings deposits remain anonymous for Austrian residents). Deregulation of the banking sector is thus largely completed. Since 1990, banks have engaged in a flurry of merger activity (as elsewhere in Europe) in order to prepare for the intensified competition of the internal market. This process of consolidation is expected to continue. Also, bank competition is expected to increase via technological change. These factors should lead to greater efficiency and thus reduced costs for users of banking services.

Insurance

As in banking, the insurance market structure is one of oligopolistic competition. The insurance sector is already highly internationalised: as of 1990, around 60 per cent of Austrian insurance firms were controlled by German parent firms, reflecting high levels of direct investment inflows over the previous decade; concentration at the same time grew markedly as the five largest firms gained market share. Also, functional or financial ties between banks and insurance firms increased, as banks made "strategic investments" in the insurance (especially life) industry. Merger and acquisition activity did not increase significantly in anticipation of the internal market in the early 1990s, however, as it did in other countries and in the Austrian banking sector; observed industry growth reflected, rather, large hikes in insurance premiums, which added considerably to inflation pressures in 1991-93. Despite the internationalisation of the sector, price competition was virtually absent due to the very tight regulatory regime, with prices remaining substantially higher in Austria than abroad.

Competition is set to rise markedly with the internal market, however. With the formation of the EEA, the Insurance Law has been amended (*VAG-Novelle* 1992) to conform with EU rules. Now, insurers from other EU countries are free to set up branches (more easily than formerly) and to provide insurance services in Austria, while Austrian firms are free to do likewise in other member countries (always in conformity with the home country's laws). To this end, former restrictive licensing requirements for market entry (*Genehmigungspflicht*), such as "proof of market need" or payment of a caution, have been eliminated. Elimination of such market-entry restrictions implies the possibility for greater domestic price competition, with faster expansion of new products and suppliers. In the longer run, insurance prices may also fall as service prices in general (including the cost of damage repair) decline in response to greater competition. The potential for further economies of scale, on the other hand, is probably limited due to the already high level of market concentration.

Road transport

Competition in road transport is low despite the pressure of a large number of firms. Concentration and internationalisation of the sector are also low. These characteristics may be traced to the fact that domestic activity is regulated by the restrictive *Gewerbeordnung* and by the *Güterbeförderungsgesetz* (Transport Law). Market entry traditionally required a concession, which was granted only upon furnishing of a qualification certificate and "proofs" of market need and performance ability. With the entry into force of the EEA Agreement Austria took over approximately 90 per cent of existing EU rules in the field of road transport, including those on qualifications and performance ability for access to the profession. The remaining 10 per cent mainly concerned market access, which between Austria and EU Member states was – until 31 December 1994 – governed by the Transit Agreement, and between Austria and the other contracting parties to the EEA Agreement by bilateral agreements. Traffic with other European countries was and still is subject to bilateral agreements.

The EU deregulated road transport as of 1993. For environmental reasons, special conditions for transit traffic of heavy goods vehicles through Austria were however set up by the Transit Agreement concluded between Austria and the EU. According to the provisions of this Agreement, a so-called "eco-point-system" was established for transit traffic of EU and Austrian vehicles through Austria, which continues to apply after the entry into force on 1 January 1995 of Protocol No. 9 of the Access Treaty on road, rail, and combined transport in Austria: each time a vehicle passes through Austria, it needs a certain number of eco-points according to its exhaust emissions: each year the global number of eco-points available is reduced by a certain percentage. This arrangement will end on 1 January 2004 (unless the target of a 60 per cent reduction in emissions of NOx from 1991 levels is achieved in an ecological and lasting way three years earlier). The 38-ton limit for vehicles (+5 per cent tolerance) continues to apply and the reciprocal quota system for bilateral traffic between Austria and the other EU Member states remains in place until 1 January 1997. Thus cross-border competition remains regulated and Austrian firms' access to fast-liberalising European markets is limited until the end of 1996.[74]

Construction

Most firms in the construction sector are small to medium sized, mainly serving the local market. Market concentration is low, as large firms control a much smaller market share than in most other countries. Even Austria's largest firms are small in international terms, while capitalisation is low throughout the sector. Internationalisation of the sector, however, is substantial and rising. Foreign (mainly German) parent firms own 20 per cent of Austrian (mainly large) firms. Austrian ownership of foreign firms has also picked up sharply since the beginning of the 1990s, largely due to purchases of Eastern German firms. Nevertheless, competition intensity is not strong. Demand is heavily influenced by government spending and procurement policies, as roughly one-third of all orders arise directly or indirectly from the public sector. Construction firms are subject to the Gewerbeordnung and as of 1992 construction was among the sectors requiring concessions to operate.

In order to conform to EU rules, Austria has been required to loosen regulation of the construction industry, adapt building standards to EU construction guidelines, and liberalise government procurement policies. The *Gewerberechtsnovelle* 1992 lifted the concession requirement for the construction sector, placing it under the less restrictive approval regime. In general this law realised the principle of free settlement and free service according to EEA-treaty and EU-membership. This gives foreigners from other EU countries the right to establish branches in Austria or to offer services from their bases abroad. Protection of the domestic market from outside competition is thereby greatly lessened. Foreigners have to meet standards of qualification comparable to certification requirements still required of Austrians; in case they do not come up to the Austrian standard they have to undergo further examination.[75] In 1993, a new law on government procurement was passed, bringing Austria largely into conformity with the EU guidelines. The earlier practice by local governments of giving preference to locally-based firms (80 per cent of the awards went to firms within an 80 kilometre radius of the awarding local authority), is no longer possible. Now, contracts above a certain minimum must be advertised Europe-wide. But Austria (along with France and Germany) maintains a difference with the general EU practice: instead of the "best price" principle, the "best supplier" principle (price-quality relationship) will be applied. Both competition and market concentration are likely to increase in the new environment, although changes are expected to come about only slowly, in part judging from the experience of other EU countries.

Wholesale and retail trade

The structure of the distribution system is one of monopolistic competition, although internationalisation is high. Foreign direct investment inflows accelerated with anticipation of EU membership, though outflows to the EU grew even faster. Both trends reflected merger and takeover activity in preparation for competition in the internal market, undertaken to secure new financing sources, diversify risks, exploit scale economies, and gain know-how on foreign markets. There was also substantial merger activity among domestic firms themselves, mainly in the form of horizontal voluntary co-operation agreements (where sales remain decentralised but purchases, advertising, financing, management and training, etc. are centralised). Market concentration has thus grown rapidly. Nonetheless, the largest firm size remains small by international terms.[76]

Margins in retail and wholesale trade exceed those in Germany, which are themselves high relative to the EU average (Table 26). The reasons for this are complex, but the relative lack of larger firms may play a role, as margins are

Table 26. **Distribution margins in Austria and Germany**
In per cent of sectoral GDP

	Wholesale		Retail	
	Austria	Germany	Austria	Germany
1980	..	..	28.7	28.1
1983	18.6	13.2	29.7	28.4
1988	21.0	16.8	30.6	28.4

Source: Breuss (1994).

observed to decline with firm size, implying a high potential for further economies of scale (Annex Table A6). Price levels are also higher than in the EU at large, especially in the household equipment, recreational and cultural goods, and food sectors (Diagram 20 above).[77] With over 100 laws and ordinances governing activity in the distribution sector, the link between high prices and regulation is evident, though almost impossible to quantify. Market entry barriers enshrined in Austrian law, such as certificates of qualification requirements, licensing and franchising, have tended to push up costs and prices by engendering inefficiencies and rent-seeking. Zoning laws limit number and size of stores, leading to a relative lack of supermarkets and discount stores. The Local Supply Law and store-closing regulations have further reduced price competition and consumer welfare.

The entry of Austria into the EEA and the EU however implies fundamental changes in the regulatory landscape, and changes have already been made. The 1993 amendment to the *Gewerbeordnung* eased entry barriers: required experience was reduced to one year (from two) and could be replaced by specialised training such as business school; trades formerly restricted by the need for operating franchises now face only the qualification certification requirements.[78] Also, Länder zoning laws are to be made EU-conforming. Laws restricting price competition and other aspects of business conduct have also been liberalised: regulations laying down a "local customary price" or prohibiting sales at less than the "initial price" have been abolished; comparative advertising is now allowed for like goods; rebates are permitted; and extended opening hours are now in force one night per week and one Saturday per month.[79] The amended Cartel Law allows a more liberal interpretation of "market-controlling firms" and simplified rules for vertical distribution arrangements.

The full impact of competitive pressure from the EEA and EU is yet to come, however:

- The elimination of customs borders, technical standardisation, and the allowance of parallel imports offer arbitrage opportunities which should reduce cross-country price differences and make price discrimination more difficult. Indeed, under EU competition law and cartel law, which is based on the prohibition principle rather than on the much weaker abuse of market power principle underlying previous Austrian law, customary practices such as exclusive supplier and sales arrangements, forbidding of parallel imports and exports, dividing up the market and territorial protection, become (in principle) illegal.[80]

– Freedom to establish branches anywhere in the internal market means that there are no discriminatory rules against foreign firms from other EU countries any longer. As qualification certification requirements remain in force for Austrian firms, there may be a need for further reform of the *Gewerbeordnung*. The easing of market entry should not only lead to more price competition, but also enable greater economies of scale (mainly in retail) and scope (mainly in wholesale, where the warehouse concept could be developed), and hence, lower costs in the distribution sector.

At the same time, the application of the EU common external tariff and common agricultural policies will lower import and farm-gate prices. The full pass-through of such price reductions will, however, require greater monitoring of competition in the distribution sector by the competition authority.

Industry

As far as the manufacturing sector is concerned, the impact of EU entry should be liberalising and trade-creating. Free trade within the EEA was still hampered by EU rules of origin restrictions, meaning that Austrian goods that were partially processed in Eastern Europe but finished in Austria faced trade restrictions when crossing customs barriers for export into the EU. With Austria a member of the EU, all customs barriers *vis-à-vis* other EU countries are eliminated, and this problem vanishes. Also, adoption of the EU's external trade policies regarding third countries may be considered a liberalising move insofar as Austria's post-Uruguay Round weighted import tariff in industry would have been higher than that of the CCT (Annex Table A7).[81] The importance of non-tariff barriers is difficult to quantify, and both the EU maintain NTBs on trade with Eastern Europe. However, Austria's policies do not appear to be more liberal than the EU's.[82]

Quantification of the economic impact of EU membership

The Austrian Institute for Economic Research (WIFO) has estimated that, by the year 2000, the impact of EU membership will be to lower the CPI by $3\frac{1}{4}$ percentage points (in addition to a 2 per cent reduction accruing from EEA

Table 27. **The macroeconomic effects of EU entry**

	WIFO macromodel (percentage change from base "EEA" scenario)		Input-output model (percentage change from base case [1])
	1995	2000	2000
Private consumption	0.9	2.1	6.5
Public consumption	1.1	1.8	4.6
Fixed investment	2.0	9.2	5.9
Exports	1.1	3.0	2.0
Imports	1.8	2.9	4.2
GDP	0.8	2.8	4.4
Private consumption deflator	−1.8	−3.3	−4.5
Terms of trade, goods	−0.4	−0.3	..
Disposable real income	2.1	3.4	..
Wage rate	−0.3	−0.2	..
Dependent employment	0.2	1.3	1.4
Labour productivity	0.7	1.4	3.0
Current account as a per cent of GDP	−0.9	−1.7	..
Net lending of general government, as a per cent of GDP	−1.5	−0.9	..

1. Assuming neither EEA nor EU membership.
Source: Breuss *et al.* (1994), Richter (1993).

participation), and to raise real GDP by 2¾ per cent (compared with a 2¼ per cent rise due to the EEA alone) (Table 27).[83] While more than 10 000 jobs are expected to be lost in those sectors with structural problems such as distribution, food processing, and agriculture, 50 000 jobs will be created in construction and other services, machinery manufacturing, tourism, and real estate. Broadly similar results are obtained with an input-output model of the Federal Economic Chamber. The expected effect of EEA participation and EU membership combined is a generalised price reduction of 4½ per cent, a GDP increase of 4½ per cent, and a net job gain of 45 000. In this simulation, virtually every sector makes net gains (except for the tobacco industry), with a considerably stronger effect in services than in manufactures, especially in financial services, communications, construction, and other (mainly professional) services (Table 28). That the growth effects would be higher in the service-producing industries than in manu-

97

Table 28.   **The effect of the internal market on the services sector, 2000** [1]

	Economies of scale	Economies of scope	Deregulation	Shift from monopoly or oligopoly structure toward full competition	Liberalisation of government procurement	Effect on real output, per cent
Banks and insurance	X	X	X	X		9.1
Transport and post						8.5
Road transport	X	X				
Air transport	X	X	X	X		
Telecommunications			X	X		
Construction	X			X	X	5.6
Miscellaneous services	X		X	X		5.7
Trade			X	X		3.9
Tourism			X	X		3.3

1.   Difference in real output with EU entry on 1 January 1995 from base scenario assuming neither EU entry nor EEA participation.

Source: Richter (1993), p. 78; Breuss (1994).

facturing is intuitively plausible, given that the deregulatory impact of the internal market will be greater in the services sector. By contrast, manufacturing sectors were already well-integrated into the EU markets with a much more competitive structure (although *de facto* trade liberalisation arising from EU membership could have significant impacts which may not be adequately accounted for in the latter simulation).

Summary and agenda for further reform

The above analysis suggests that Austria's good overall economic performance, based on strong labour productivity growth, a low unemployment rate, relatively stable manufacturing-sector employment and moderate inflation, is in danger of being undermined by several potentially detrimental structural features:

–   favourable overall productivity performance has been associated with relatively low rates of return on investment, slow TFP growth, inadequate innovation and a failure adequately to exploit economies of scale and scope;

- the low unemployment rate has co-existed with a rather inadequate pace of job creation and productivity growth in the service sectors;
- the high proportion of employment in manufacturing is surprising in the light of revealed comparative disadvantage in goods trade;
- Austrian prices have remained relatively high because of the lack of competition in the sheltered sectors, as well as the small size of the home market which limited the possible economies of scale and scope.

With respect to low TFP growth, the analysis above has highlighted several factors related to the capital market which might help to explain both the relatively small degree of new firm creation and the failure fully to exploit the potential for scale economies. At the same time, the process of innovation and research needed to develop a more important presence in the technology-intensive areas of trade may not be best served by the vocationally-oriented education system. Most importantly, the preponderance of manufacturing, and the relative underdevelopment of the service sector are due to entry restrictions and excessive regulation in the sheltered sectors at large, as well as a general lack of competition. As a result, the proportion of people employed in the service sectors is relatively low and prices high. As the economy opens up to Eastern Europe, the Austrian manufacturing sector is likely to meet with increased competition, particularly given its specialisation pattern in low-technology and labour-intensive goods. Austria's manufacturing specialisations will thus need to change, and resources set free in contracting sectors will need to be reallocated elsewhere, calling for the abolition of restrictions and enhanced competition in the service sectors. In this respect, EU entry will be helpful, having already given rise to a number of liberalisation measures and enhancing competition from abroad. But, domestic policy initiatives will also be needed in the fields of capital market and development and education, together with initiatives to reinforce the ongoing process of regulatory and institutional reform.

Capital market and human capital development

Capital market reform has begun in earnest, with results yet to be seen. However, more might be done to boost the development of capital markets, especially for equities:

- The existing pension scheme discourages the formation of private pension funded schemes, which in other countries serve as major ''fuel'' for stock and bond markets. Allowing such plans to develop through appropriate policy changes would not only help to stimulate capital markets but also address future problems in pension system finance (see Part II).

- The setting up of an independent stock market supervisory authority is an important next step in promoting market transparency and boosting investor confidence. This could be an authority similar to the German *"Wertpapieraufsichtsamt"*. Corresponding to the security-services regulations of the EU, the establishment of such a body is currently under discussion.
- In general, as elsewhere, the problem is to ensure that smaller firms have the financial resources for growth. In this respect, greater venture capital may be needed. Further reducing interest subsidies, which discriminate against smaller companies, would also be helpful.

Less progress has been made in strengthening the *human capital* base. Apprenticeship programmes are in need of updating and better quality control is necessary to ensure that marketable skills are being imparted. There is also the need to shift toward more tertiary education. In this respect, the government's proposal to build more *Fachhochschulen* is promising and should be accompanied by an expansion of university capacity and quality (see last year's *Survey*). Given the public-good nature of basic research, continued government funding of university research is appropriate in this area, but better quality controls on such assistance need to be introduced.

Deregulation and institutional reform

The analysis in this chapter has also underlined the importance of product-market deregulation in Austria, where the service sector is relatively underdeveloped and the "excess burden" of inadequate competition on consumer prices very high. EU membership and budgetary pressures are likely to have important effects here, but the pace of reform may in some cases be too gradual. As an example, a highly competitive *telecommunications sector* is critical to innovation and economic growth, being a requirement for the "information based economy" and having important spill-over effects into high-tech manufacturing. Telecommunications services are in any event a critical element of the business sector infrastructure and are a major cost component affecting overall competitiveness. However, development of the sector remains largely at Austria's own initiative. At a minimum, management of the telephone monopoly should be made autonomous from budget considerations, with free access to financial markets for the undertaking of investments.[84] Also, entry to network services by private sector competitors must be allowed. In this sector, the arguments for privatisation are relatively strong. Indeed, in the case of privatisation, the indirect benefits to the budget arising from greater economic efficiency and growth should easily outweigh the direct loss of receipts.

In *distribution*, liberalisation ahead of EU membership has not yet had a significant impact on observed competition; in any event the trading sector is still heavily regulated. In other service sectors, progress has been made towards freer markets, but much remains to be done if the job-creating potential of these sectors is to be exploited. EU membership alone cannot be counted on to automatically solve all the problems in this sector, and even poses new challenges to the traditional institutions, including the chamber system, on which the principle of the social partnership is based. EU entry is, in this respect, prompting questions about the need for a shift from co-operation and administration to new tasks, such as adaptation of the labour force to challenges from the east and west and the active promotion of competition in product markets.

Conclusions

The recovery in the Austrian economy became increasingly firmly established in the course of 1994 with exports of goods, the usual motor of recovery, particularly buoyant. More than in the past, the upturn has also been driven by growth of fixed investment; having shown considerable resilience during the downturn, consumption, both private and public, has been slower to pick up. Overall, the relatively shallow recession once again confirmed the ability of the Austrian economy to weather international storms, due in large measure to the high degree of aggregate wage flexibility in Austria. Lower wage increases, in conjunction with a cyclical recovery in productivity, brought unit labour costs almost to a standstill in 1994. Partly as a result, unemployment began to fall unusually early in the recovery, although the initial rapid fall seems to have given way to a more gradual improvement. Output is recovering faster than potential growth, and Austria may have less spare capacity than most other European countries.

The economy seems set to continue this robust performance over the coming two years, GDP growth consolidating in the region of 3 per cent a year. With an ongoing recovery elsewhere in Europe, export markets are likely to remain buoyant and the combination of steady output growth, healthy profits and the confidence effects of EU accession should sustain growth of investment. Despite an improving labour market situation, domestic consumption may continue to lag behind other demand components due, chiefly, to the short-term impact of phasing in the new government's fiscal stabilisation plan. Inflation may fall in 1995 – if only because EU membership entails lower food prices. Further ahead, in 1996, there is, however, a risk of a rebound in inflationary pressure against the background of a gradual absorption of economic slack.

The Austrian business cycle being closely aligned to that of Germany, interest rates will tend to follow German rates up as the output gap closes in both countries, the link with the Deutschemark continuing to form the basis for sustained, healthy growth over the medium term. This policy has served Austria well, establishing an anchor for inflation expectations and thereby helping to provide a stable framework for private-sector decision making. Reflecting the general credibility of this approach, Austrian interest rates no longer contain a premium over German rates. Though the institutional framework has changed with Austria's membership of the Exchange Rate Mechanism of the European Monetary System, the fixed exchange-rate link with Germany can, and should, be continued, providing an essential underpinning to stability-oriented monetary policy. If anything, with the increasingly close relationship between the German and Austrian economies, the appropriateness of the exchange-rate link has increased over time.

Nevertheless, insofar as there are indications that the more buoyant economic climate is bringing wage disinflation to a halt, leaving inflation higher than the OECD average, progress on price disinflation has been disappointing. Higher indirect taxes and publicly-controlled prices are among the reasons for slow disinflation. However, stubborn inflation has also been caused by increased rents and widening profit margins, repeating the pattern that when other inflation components shrink profits grow more strongly. This tendency, besides reflecting the usual cyclical pattern, seems also to derive from structural problems, including lack of competition, that affect the sheltered sector of the economy. These problems go beyond what is amenable to monetary policy, and need to be addressed through structural reform, a matter which is further discussed below.

A further symptom of structural imbalance may be the current account deficit. With the Austrian economy recovering relatively rapidly and imports reacting more rapidly than domestic supply, the external balance continued its negative trend in 1994. The overall deficit remained relatively small and was readily financeable. Moreover, the external balance corresponds to the excess of domestic investment over domestic saving and though both rose in 1994, the rise in investment was the faster; seen in this light, the deficit should not be a cause for worry, provided that saving and investment are guided by sound incentives. However, two features of the rising external deficit qualify this sanguine view. First, the decline in the surplus on tourism, traditionally a source of finance for the large trade deficit, is perhaps symptomatic of structural problems in the service sector of the domestic economy already noted above. And second, the trend towards a widening deficit has as a domestic counterpart a rising public sector deficit.

Since 1993, fiscal policy has been following a course which would be unsustainable if left uncorrected. The deviation from the original medium-term plan has raised questions concerning budgetary management and control, some of which have been addressed by recent reforms to the budgetary process. These reforms include, most notably, the setting of multi-year budget targets, the monitoring of actual relative to targeted developments and the obligation to correct overruns. Better public expenditure control, along the lines set out in the 1994 *Survey*, is all the more important since from 1995 contributions to the EU budget will imply an additional, and substantial, budgetary burden, as will transitional support for Austrian agriculture. Even abstracting from the costs of EU entry, programmed expenditure increases threaten to exceed revenue growth under existing tax structures and rates.

Against that background, the new Government has proposed a comprehensive fiscal programme with the aim of bringing down the general government deficit to a level consistent with the 3 per cent deficit ceiling set out in the Maastricht treaty. This target is to be achieved within the current legislative period and with the main emphasis put on expenditure cuts over a broad range of areas, through increases in taxes also play a role. Proposed measures incorporated in the 1995 Budget include savings on the government wage bill, cuts in transfers related to family policy, initiatives to raise the effective pension age, and higher taxes on mineral oil products.

Two questions arise in the context of the new programme. First, are the proposed measures consistent with the stated target? and, second, is the target sufficiently ambitious? Concerning the first question, and continuing a long Austrian tradition, many of the details of the programme have still to be worked out in co-operation with the social partners; until the exact content of the programme and the time schedule for its implementation are known, it is difficult to give an accurate assessment. The reality is, however, that if the government's budgetary goals are to be attained and increases in tax pressures minimised, painful decisions on public spending will have to be made. Concerning the second question, it would be unfortunate if the fiscal consolidation objectives were met only because the economy happened to be at a cyclical peak. Indeed, the deficit target should be interpreted with reference to the state of the cycle, implying the need for some over-fulfilment were output to exceed its potential level, in order to pre-empt any subsequent overshooting as the economy turned down. More fundamentally, in view of the future challenges posed by an ageing population, a higher level of ambition with respect to deficit reduction may be warranted. It should also be borne in mind that, even after the full introduction of the programme, public expenditure levels will remain high, reflecting, *inter alia,* still-generous social transfer provisions in many areas.

The need for fiscal consolidation underlines the need for better use of available labour resources, since these set the limit for the sustainable recovery of output and thereby the cyclical improvement of the budget. There are two issues here, which are also important in their own right. First, the fact that unemployment in Austria is relatively low is not apparently due to its being less persistent than in European high-unemployment countries: as elsewhere unemployment tends to ratchet up in the wake of each cyclical downturn. Low unemployment seems, rather, to be explained by the fact that unemployment typically has risen relatively little during downturns. The buffering role that migration has played in the past is probably among the explanations for this stability of unemployment. But a new and more restrictive immigration regime may reduce this effect in the future.

Second, low unemployment is not associated with a particularly high level of employment. Rather, important segments of the population have much lower rates of activity than in comparable countries. This is the case for older persons for instance, the average effective pension age having fallen as low as fifty-eight. Among the reasons for this are the generosity of early retirement and invalidity pensions, combined, in the case of the latter, with relatively light control. The new fiscal programme contains provisions to deal with these problems and it is important that these provisions should not be diluted in the process of implementation. Indeed, further measures may be necessary in these areas. Female labour force participation is also not particularly high. Apart from disincentives arising from the transfer system, this is likely to reflect the low availability of part-time work. This may again be traced back to the regulations and restrictions which have hampered the development of the service sector.

More generally, Austria's low and relatively stable unemployment rate may be traced to the high degree of aggregate wage flexibility which is a product of the particular institutional features of the Austrian labour market, the pervasive influence of the social partners in the stabilisation process being a hallmark of the "Austrian model". In this context, new challenges have arisen with the opening up of Eastern Europe and the membership of the EU – challenges that are likely to call for an intensified transfer of resources between sectors, firms and occupations. In the new and more competitive environment, flexibility including that of relative wages, will become more important than it has been in the past. This will call for the social partnership to adapt to new challenges by introducing more flexibility at the micro level, while continuing to rely on the strengths of the existing institutional set-up at an aggregate level.

As in other OECD countries, the manufacturing sector in Austria has been shrinking. This is partly a result of efforts begun in the mid-1980s to reform and (ultimately) privatise the nationalised industries, but increased rationalisation is also occurring in private industry in response to intensified international competition. However, as in much of OECD Europe, service sector expansion has been hampered by high barriers to entry and lack of competition. Low enterprise entry and exit rates also indicate a relative lack of dynamism. If these trends continue, structural unemployment could ratchet up to unacceptable levels. Hence, the key objective of structural reform should be to increase the job-creating potential of services, while creating the conditions for industry to adapt to new competitive challenges.

Austria's pattern of specialisation within OECD manufacturing, emphasising resource- and labour-intensive production to the relative neglect of science-based and other higher value-added production, makes it vulnerable to emerging competition from Eastern Europe and also East Asia. Austria is not alone in being dependent on low-technology industries, but the competitive challenge facing it may be more acute than elsewhere, because of its much higher trade exposure to eastern Europe. Nevertheless, Austria's long-term interests would be best served by working toward the removal of EU non-tariff barriers against the eastern European economies and the further integration of these countries with Europe. A wealthier Eastern Europe arising from freer access to EU markets and greater freedom of factor flows can only improve Austria's own welfare and economic security. By the same token, the potential advantages of growing trade and investment linkages with Eastern Europe are high, and probably much higher than most empirical studies would suggest. Such advantages include large terms of trade gains deriving from access to these countries' low labour and resource costs; new and growing markets for Austrian exports, and productivity gains arising from the development of alternative patterns of specialisation, based on more effective use of Austria's financial and human resources.

To maximise the net gains from trade with Eastern Europe and indeed other non-OECD countries, an unhindered flow of resources – both financial and human – into more innovative and higher-value added activities is needed. There is some evidence that the innovative capacity of the Austrian business sector is limited by distortions in the allocation of capital and insufficient availability of R&D and production skills. As a result, R&D spending is low and total factor productivity growth weak. Policy priorities in these areas are the development of effective equity and venture capital markets; completing the elimination of distorting credit subsidies; improved quality controls in the funding of university research and vocational training programmes; a greater emphasis on post-secondary education, and better advice and infrastructure support especially to smaller firms.

As regards competition in the service sector, EU membership should help to open up several formerly sheltered sectors such as telecommunications, distribution, construction, and professional services. This will allow for easier entry of new firms, and hence more competition, and for the growth of existing firms, giving greater economies of scale and scope. Moreover, enhanced competition as a result of EU membership should help put an end to anti-competitive practices, thereby reducing currently high profit margins and limiting price discrimination. Austria has already enacted a large number of policy reforms in line with EU guidelines to ease entry and promote competition. But the experience of countries already within the EU – where expected welfare gains from the internal market have often taken longer than expected to materialise – suggests that the impact of market opening depends on the support of domestic policies. This implies that further reforms, involving extensive privatisation of state enterprises in telecommunications and other areas and reaching into the social partnership may be inevitable. In particular, the pressure on the Chambers to adapt to changing industrial circumstances so as to permit a more rapid reallocation of labour across sectors, would seem to call for a review of their current rigid membership structure.

In sum, the future contains important challenges both for policy makers and for the business sector itself. However, these challenges should be viewed positively. Judged by conventional macroeconomic indicators, the Austrian economy has so far been among the better performers in the OECD. There are signs that, prior to entry into the EU, this relatively favourable position was being eroded in some respects and EU membership should go part way to correcting this trend, by opening up the economy to greater competition, reducing regulatory hindrances and increasing the flexibility of response to the challenge to the East. Provided also that appropriate action is also taken to deal with the fiscal imbalance, there is no reason why the economy should not exploit these benefits effectively while building on its traditional strengths.

Notes

1. With German travel expenditure up by around 6 per cent in nominal terms in the first half of 1994 compared to a year earlier, there is some indication of a shift in destinations away from Austria. Partly, this may reflect that tourism in Austria typically has catered for German low-wage earners and that this group has been particularly affected by weak real incomes and may have fewer financial resources allowing a smoothing of consumption patterns.

2. On some calculations, the fixed capital stock per worker in Austria now corresponds to that of the United States though it remains lower than in Germany (Englander and Gurney, 1994).

3. Some main features of the Austrian housing market were presented in the 1990/91 *Survey*.

4. See Aiginger *et al.*, 1994.

5. A number of stylised facts concerning Austrian business cycles are discussed in Rünstler (1994).

6. OECD estimates of import equations for manufactures suggest that the elasticity of imports with respect to trend demand growth is about unity but that demand deviations relative to trend affect imports with a semi-elasticity of 2.6 – one of the highest among the smaller OECD countries.

7. There are indications that travel expenditure may contain payments that properly belong to other parts of the current account or even the capital account.

8. This includes expenditure on services purchased abroad in connection with civil engineering projects abroad.

9. Over the period 1984-92, more than 60 per cent of the variation in Austrian GDP growth can be explained by coincident and one quarter lagged German GDP growth – up from about 30 per cent between the mid-1970s and the mid-1980s (Rünstler, 1994).

10. Unemployed persons committed to re-enter their previous job at the following seasonal upturn are not regarded as unemployed in the survey. Comparing across countries, only Belgium, where the number of benefit recipients exceed the survey-based number of unemployed by 48 per cent, has a larger discrepancy than the 32 per cent in Austria (1991) (OECD, 1994*a*).

11. See Bundesministerium für Arbeit und Soziales (1994).

12. Measured relative to transit exports, the transit balance represents a "value added" of, on average, about 12 per cent. However, this figure includes also costs related to freight etc. (Stankovsky, 1994).

13. See Schneider (1994).

14. See Breuss *et al.* (1994).

15. For example third country imports of computers, faxes and camera equipment which were previously free of customs duty will be subject to the common EU tariff ranging from 4.4 to 7.2 per cent. In surveys of retail trade, about a third of respondents have indicated that EU-induced price falls would not be passed on to consumers.

16. See OECD (1994).

17. On an administrative basis, there was a Sch 24 billion overrun for the federal deficit, the main causes for which were an unforeseen Sch 7 billion net reserves build-up plus Sch 8½ billion in loan disbursements, which boosted the borrowing requirement on top of that arising from the overrun on cash basis.

18. A large rise in transfers to enterprises in the 1994 budget was due to the corporatisation and separation from the budget of ÖBB. To put subsidisation in perspective, a recent government report has estimated that indirect subsidies due to tax expenditure may be about three times higher than direct subsidies.

19. Growth of potential output is estimated at around 2¼ per cent. The calculation of potential output and the output gap are described in Annex I.

20. Combining the 1993 and 1994 observations, and assuming linearity between the extent of disinflation and net lending, an estimate of net lending at unchanged inflation can be derived on the basis that a further deceleration in inflation of 0.5 per cent is associated with an increase in the deficit of 0.3 per cent. Hence if inflation had been steady in 1994, instead of falling by 0.8 per cent, the deficit would have been 0.48 per cent of GDP lower (0.6×0.8), giving a cyclically-adjusted deficit of 3.9 per cent of GDP.

21. The official budget entry for this item of Sch 28 billion (*Table 9*) already nets out the savings on contributions to the EEA.

22. The planned draw-down of reserves amounts to Sch 17 billion, which is the major reason that on an administrative basis, the deficit declines by Sch 2½ billion, to Sch 102 billion.

23. As discussed further in Part III, unemployment in Austria seems to show the same tendencies for persistence as elsewhere in Europe, implying that the level of unemployment at which inflation begins to rise, may have increased.

24. The rate was calculated based on net interest payments relative to the gross government debt and is therefore biased downwards to the extent the government receives interest. Government assets corresponding to about 5 per cent of GDP are held in the form of bonds and bank deposits etc., *i.e.* instruments likely to give a return related to market interest rates. Also, the use of this implicit rate does not take into account that interest income accruing in the private sector is, in principle, subject to tax.

25. The semi-elasticity of 0.49 corresponds closely to the unweighted average of 0.50 across OECD countries, see Annex I.

26.   Insofar as debt is reduced this way, debt interest payments will evidently also be reduced and the deficit will be lowered. Given the low return the government is currently receiving on its assets, the revenue side of government budgets is unlikely to be seriously affected.

27.   These calculations are relatively sensitive to the assumption concerning the real rate of interest. If the real interest rate were assumed to be $4\frac{1}{4}$ per cent instead of $3\frac{3}{4}$ per cent, the cumulative deficit in the "neutral" and "no change" scenarios would be some $1\frac{1}{2}$ per cent of GDP higher and the cuts needed to respect the Maastricht deficit criterion would be correspondingly larger.

28.   For time-series evidence and evidence based on wage equations, see Elmeskov and Macfarlan (1994).

29.   However, in 1990-91, a further reduction of unemployment may have been hindered by a strong influx of foreign workers (some 110 000 persons).

30.   See Pichelmann (1994) and Elmeskov and Pichelmann (1993).

31.   For details, see Elmeskov and Pichelmann (1994).

32.   Among the countries considered in Elmeskov (1993), Austria is the only country to have experienced a rise in the seasonality of unemployment over the period since the early 1970s.

33.   The Austrian UI system implies no experience rating for either employers or employees. However, as mentioned in Part II the new government's fiscal programme signals an intention to modify the existing set of rules in this area.

34.   Sectoral analysis of unemployment changes among OECD economies suggests that shifts in manufacturing employment have a disproportionately large impact on unemployment trends (Glyn and Rowthorn, 1988). More generally, unemployment in OECD countries seems to respond more strongly to sectoral employment declines than to corresponding increases but such employment shake-outs, which in other countries affected mainly manufacturing, have probably been less important in Austria (Elmeskov, 1993).

35.   The relatively low proportion of part-time work in Austria (7.7 per cent of total employment), implies that, relative to other countries, a participation rate based on number of persons employed tends to understate the potential number of productive work hours.

36.   This estimate is highly uncertain and only corresponds to about the size of the standard error of estimation.

37.   See Table 5.3 in OECD (1990a). Government-run kindergartens are currently being subsidised and a targeted scheme for child-care support aimed at unemployed women also exists.

38.   The tax system may also act as a disincentive. Though the income tax unit in Austria is the individual person, the single earner's tax credit is disallowed if the income of the spouse exceeds a certain level, resulting in a general disincentive for female participation (Silhavy, 1993). The income threshold for this tax credit being fairly low, it may particularly affect part-time work. In addition, the maximum special expense allowance (*Sonderausgabe*) is split equally between two working spouses. This may entail a lower value of tax deductions for repayments of housing and certain other loans, certain insurance premiums and other items compared to a single earner.

39. Similarly, that Austrian men have the lowest part-time frequency in the OECD area, at 1½ per cent, is no proof of any inherent discrimination against part-time work. Low female participation rates may force married men to work full-time to a higher extent than elsewhere.

40. Female participation across countries is generally positively related to the share of service sector employment (OECD, 1994).

41. See Biffl (1992).

42. This relates to the replacement rate under the general old-age pension system. The calculation was made under the rules prevailing in 1989 (OECD, 1992). Since then, the base period for calculation of pension has been increased from ten to fifteen years.

43. See OECD (1994b).

44. Hauptverband der Österreichischen Sozialversicherungsträger (1993). A tightening of the procedures for obtaining disability pension is part of the new fiscal programme (see Part II).

45. The notion that immigrants just displace native workers received very little support in a recent study based on microdata (Winter-Ebmer and Zweimüller, 1994).

46. This result is obtained by deflating nominal growth of gross fixed investment in this sector by the increase in the overall business investment deflator.

47. See OECD (1993), Diagram 10.

48. The rise in the producer price index – a better indicator of underlying inflation performance as it avoids the complication of compositional shifts – was low for chemicals over the same period.

49. On the other hand, a recent study by the WIFO (Hahn 1994) has shown *total economy* TFP growth during the 1980s similar to that of Germany, Belgium, and the Netherlands. TFP growth in manufacturing was, in fact, higher than in these other countries.

50. In 1992, Austria displayed a 26 per cent investment to GDP share, compared with 20½ per cent for the OECD on average.

51. See Hutschenreiter (1994).

52. Recent OECD studies have in fact shown that it is not enough for a country to acquire scientific and technological knowledge from outside; it must have a certain level of scientific expertise of its own if it is to take full advantage of the economic spin-off from technological development.

53. See Leo *et al.* (1992).

54. See F. Schneider (1991) and OECD (1987).

55. See Bartel and Schneider (1991).

56. At present, the Ministry of Finance supervises the primary market, while the *"Börsenkammer"* (stock market chamber), consulting the Ministry of Finance, supervises the secondary market.

57. See Austrian National Bank (1994).

58. See OECD (1994a).

59. See OECD (1993).

60. Subsidies are mainly directed to the housing sector and thus do not directly distort resource allocation within the business sector. However, the resultant bias in favour of housing investment may act to the detriment of business sector investment as a whole. See OECD (1991).

61. See OECD (1994e), Table 4.18.

62. The graduates of such advanced-level technical colleges obtain, after three years of professional practice, the title of engineer.

63. See OECD (1994d), Table 3.A.1.

64. Outflows to Western Europe countries also rose sharply in response to Austria's application for EU membership status in 1989, as firms sought to establish footholds in the EU (see below).

65. There are other important linkages as well. Immigration inflows have risen, mainly war refugees from the former Yugoslavia. Also, among all OECD countries, Austria maintains the densest network of bilateral agreements with the eastern European countries in the fields of trade, co-operation, investment protection, and the elimination of double taxation.

66. However, there is also an important segment of direct investment whose main motive is to be in a position to control the new Eastern markets to the benefit of Austrian exporters.

67. The theory of factor-price equalisation predicts that, over time, these initial relative price differences will tend to disappear. This implies that trade forces countries to seek out new opportunities for comparative advantage continuously.

68. For example, a study by the WIFO (Kramer, Peneder and Stankovsky, 1992), which relies on a partial equilibrium analysis, predicts net job creation of about 15 000 over the medium-run. A study by the Institute for Higher Studies (Wörtgötter, 1993) obtains, on the basis of simulation of its large-scale macroeconomic model, a net job gain of 50 000. Another study by Andersen and Dittus (1994) concludes that trade growth will lead to employment losses in Austria and elsewhere in the EU even with balanced trade because of the higher labour intensity of imports than of exports. In their study, the gross employment impact of a doubling of central-East European exports in the "sensitive" sectors is much higher in Austria than in those EU countries with relatively large proportions of employment in such sectors (such as Spain and Portugal), due to the far higher existing trade exposure of Austria.

69. See EC Commission (1993).

70. Rail transport is not discussed, as it was analysed extensively in last year's *Survey*. Energy distribution, air transport, and the liberal professions, are also not treated.

71. Regarding telephone services, the PTV installs the first telephone for new connections, but additional telephones on the same line may be purchased from private sources. The installation of equipment for the telephone network has also been fully liberalised since 1988. Government officials (ministry of public works and transportation) control the issuing of communications licenses.

72. See OECD (1995).

73. See EC Commission (1993).

74. EU membership also has impacts in the area of taxation. According to the provisions of an EU directive, Austria has considerably raised vehicle taxes, which were formerly below the EU minimum level, and replaced the former *"Straßenverkehrsbeitrag"* (a per ton and kilometre monthly levy) by a user charge, based on the time spent in Austria, which will be reduced step by step to the EU maximum level within the next two years.

75. The range of activities allowed on the basis of Austrian certification is unusually wide: not only construction work proper, but also planning, consultancy, and site supervision. For other countries these activities are in the purview only of architects.

76. In 1989, the largest European retail firms had more than 5 times the turnover of the largest Austrian firm, and Austria does not figure among the top 20 European retail groups.

77. The Arbeiterkammer in 1986 estimated that prices of high value added consumer goods were 20-30 per cent higher than in Germany after adjusting for VAT differences. An EFTA study has shown similar differences from the EU average. See Breuss (1994). However, a 1986 study by the Austrian Institute of Trade Research comparing retail price levels in upper Austria and Bavaria found price differences of 15 to 20 per cent, inclusive of VAT and adjusting for the different consumption bundles.

78. The former very restrictive regulations remain in place mainly in weapons, fireworks, and tobacco distribution.

79. The "normal" weekday closing time has also been lengthened, from 18:00 hours formerly to 18:30 hours currently.

80. Nevertheless, exemptions to the EU competition law allowed in certain areas, such as autos, perfumes, photo, game, and sports supplies, and book and newspaper trade, mean that cartel-like practices – apart from the prohibition of parallel imports – can be maintained in such areas in some form.

81. The main reason is that Austria grants only a 50 per cent tariff preference to eastern European countries with which it has not concluded free trade agreements (former Soviet Union) and to other developing countries, whereas the EU grants full tariff relief (however, quotas are present). Also, the EU tariff rate applied to non-Europe OECD is on average lower than Austria's.

82. On the other hand, in the area of Japanese car imports, where the EU maintains a restrictive quota policy, Austria's policies are *de facto* less restrictive, in that a lowering of the applicable tariff rate is given in exchange for Japanese auto makers' purchases of auto parts from Austria above a certain level. Such special arrangements, though allowable under GATT rules, will not be possible in the EU. Austria is still negotiating as to its allotment in the EU's overall Japanese car import quota.

83. These simulations assume no budgetary offset to the direct and indirect budgetary costs of EU entry. Given the nature of the model, inclusion of such offsets could reduce the projected growth impacts.

84. Investment finance is governed by the Telecommunications Investment Law, which allows almost exclusively credit financing.

Bibliography

Aiginger, K., M. Czerny and K. Musil (1994), "Investitionen springen mit Konjunkturbelebung an", WIFO *Monatsberichte*, 7.

Andersen, P. and Dittus, P. (1994), "Trade and employment: can we afford better market access for eastern Europe?", Austrian National Bank.

Austrian National Bank (1994), *Austrian Financial Markets*.

Bartel, R. and Schneider, F. (1991), "The 'mess' of the public sector industrial production in Austria: a typical case of public sector inefficiency?", *Public Choice*, 68, pp. 17-40.

Beirat für Wirschafts – und Sozialfragen (1994), *Wirtschaftsstandort Österreich*, Nr. 70.

Biffl, G. (1992), "Ältere Arbeitskräfte auf dem österreichischen Arbeitsmarkt", *WIFO-Vorträge*, 58.

Brandel, F., H. Hofer, L. Lassnigg and K. Pichelmann (1994), "Aspekte der Arbeitsmarktintegration von Lehranfängern", Institute for Advanced Studies.

Breuss, F., K. Kratena and F. Schebeck (1994), "Effekte eines EC-Beitritts für die Gesamtwirtschaft und für die einzelnen Sektoren", in *Österreich in der Europäischen Union – Anforderungen und Chancen für die Wirtschaft, WIFO Monatsberichte*, Sonderheft.

Breuss, F., (1994), *Die Auswirkungen des Binnenmarktes auf den Dienstleistungssektor in Österreich*, WIFO.

Bundesministerium für Arbeit und Soziales (1994), *Arbeitsmarktvorschau 1994*.

Bundesministerium für Finanzen (1994), *Budgetprognose und Investitionsprogramm des Bundes für die Jahre 1994-1997*.

Butschek, F. (1992), *Der österreichische Arbeitsmarkt – von der Industrialiserung bis zur Gegenwart*.

EC Commission (1992), *Enterprises in Europe*, Second Report.

EC Commission (1992a), *Third Survey on State Aids*.

EC Commission (1993), "Market Services in the Community Economy", *European Economy*, Supplement A.

EC Commission (1994), *Enterprises in Europe*, Third Report.

Elmeskov, J. (1993), "High and Persistent Unemployment: Assessment of the Problem and its Causes", *OECD Economics Department Working Papers*, 132.

115

Elmeskov, J. and M. Macfarlan (1994), "Unemployment Persistence", *OECD Economic Studies*, 21.

Elmeskov, J. and K. Pichelmann (1993), "Unemployment and Labour Force Participation – Trends and Cycles", *OECD Economics Department Working Papers*, 130.

Englander, A.S. and A. Gurney (1994), "OECD Productivity Growth: Medium-term trends", *OECD Economic Studies*, 22.

Englander, A.S. and A. Gurney (1994), "Medium-term Determinants of OECD Productivity", *OECD Economic Studies*, 22.

Enzelsberger, E.F. (1994), "Was wird aus der österreichischen Sozialpartnerschaft nach dem EC-Beitritt?", *Orientierungen zur Wirtschafts- und Gesellschaftspolitik*, 61.

Giorno, C., W. Leibfritz, P. Richardson and D. Roseveare, "Estimating Potential Output, Output Gaps and Structural Budget Balances", *OECD Economics Department Working Paper*, 152.

Glyn, A. and B. Rowthorn (1988), "West European Unemployment: Corporatism and Structural Change", *American Economic Association Papers and Proceedings*.

Gros, I. (1993), "Frauenerwerbsarbeit in Österreich: Ein Überblick über die heutige Situation", in *Sozial- und Wirtschaftswissenschaftliche Aspekte: Frauen im Erwerbsleben*, Bundesministerium für Arbeit und Soziales.

Hauptverband der österreichischen Sozialversicherungsträger (1993), *Handbuch der österreichischen Sozialversicherung*.

Hochreiter, E. (editor) (1993), "The impact of the opening of the east on the Austrian economy, a first quantitative assessment", Austrian National Bank.

Hoeller, P. and Louppe, M-O. (1994), "The EC's internal market: implementation, economic consequences, unfinished business", OECD *Economics Department Working Papers* 147.

Hutschenreiter (1994), "Innovation und Produktivitätsentwicklung in der österreichischen Industrie", WIFO.

Kramer, H., M. Peneder and J. Stankovsky (1992), "Chancen und Gefährdungspotentiale der Ostöffnung: Konseguenzen für die österreichische Wirtschaft", WIFO.

Leo, H., G. Palme, and E. Volk (1992), *Die Innovationstätigkeit der österreichischen Industrie*, WIFO.

Mayerhofer, P. (1992), *Wien im neuen Mitteleuropa, ökonomische Effekte der Ostöffnung*, WIFO.

Neyer, G. (1993), "Risiko oder Sicherheit? Karenzurlaub in Österreich: Wirkungen und Tendenzen", in *Sozial- und Wirtschaftswissenschaftliche Aspekte: Frauen im Erwerbsleben*, Bundesministerium für Arbeit und Soziales.

OECD (1987), *Structural change and economic performance*.

OECD (1990), *Economic Surveys – Austria*.

OECD (1990a), *Employment Outlook*.

OECD (1992), *Employment Outlook*.

OECD (1993), *Economic Surveys – Austria*.

OECD (1993a), *Education at a Glance*.

OECD (1994), *Economic Surveys – Austria.*

OECD (1994a), *Economic Surveys – Germany.*

OECD (1994b), *OECD Economic Surveys – Netherlands.*

OECD (1994c), *Employment Outlook.*

OECD (1994d), *The OECD Jobs Study: Evidence and Explanations – Labour Market Trends and Underlying Forces of Change.*

OECD (1994e), *The OECD Jobs Study: Evidence and Explanations – The Adjustment Potential of the Labour Market.*

OECD (1995), *Communications Outlook.*

Pichelmann, K. (1994), "Konjunktur und Arbeitsmarktentwicklung", *Wirtschaftspolitische Blätter*, 41/3.

Richter, J. (1993), "Österreich und der Europäische Binnenmarkt", in Breuss, F. and Kitzmantel, E. (editors), *Die europäische Integration: Untersuchung der sektoralen Auswirkungen*, Ministry of Finance.

Rowthorn, R.E. (1992), "Centralisation, Employment and Wage Dispersion", *The Economic Journal*, 102.

Rünstler, G. (1994), "Technische Probleme von Konjunkturprognosen", *Wirtschaftspolitische Blätter*, 41/3.

Schneider, F. (1991), "Efficiency and profitability: an inverse relationship according to the size of Austrian firms?", *Small Business Economics* 3, pp. 287-296.

Schneider, M. (1994), "Chancen und Risken der Landwirtschaft im EU-Binnenmarkt", in *Österreich in der Europäischen Union – Anforderungen und Chancen für die Wirtschaft*, WIFO *Monatsberichte*, Sonderheft.

Silhavy, H. (1993), "Verschiedene Ebenen entdiskriminierender Massnahmen", in *Sozial- und Wirtschaftswissenschaftliche Aspekte: Frauen im Erwerbsleben*, Bundesministerium für Arbeit und Soziales.

Smeral, E. (1993), *Bericht Über die Lage der Tourismus-und Freizeitwirtschaft in Österreich 1993*, Der Bundesminister für wirtschaftliche Angelegenheiten.

Smeral, E. (1994a), "Tourismuspolitik 2000", Bundesministerium für wirtschaftliche Angelegenheiten.

Smeral, E. (1994b), "Tourismus 2005", WIFO in association with the Bundesministerium für wirtschaftliche Angelegenheiten.

Stankovsky, J. (1994), "Neue Funktion des österreichischen Transithandels", *WIFO Monatsberichte*, 9.

Stankovsky, J. (1994), "Österreich als Teil der EU-Zollunion", in *Österreich in der Europäischen Union – Anforderungen und Chancen für die Wirtschaft*, WIFO *Monatsberichte*, Sonderheft.

Winter-Ebmer, R. and J. Zweimüller, "Do Immigrants Displace Native Workers? The Austrian Experience", *CEPR Discussion Paper Series*, 991.

Wörtgötter, A. (1993), "Comments", in E. Hochreiter (editor), "The impact of the opening of the east on the Austrian economy: A first quantitative assessment", Austrian National Bank.

Annex I

Technical notes

Potential output and the output gap

Estimates of potential output underlie the assessments of the output gap and the cyclically-adjusted budget balance shown in the main text. The quantification of potential output is based on a production function approach.[1] Two production factors, capital and labour, are combined in a Cobb-Douglas production function to produce business sector output. Potential output in the business sector, *YPB*, is derived by combining the existing stock of capital, *KB*, with potential employment in the business sector, *EPB*, at trend total factor productivity, *TFPT*:

$$YPB = f(KB, EPB, TFPT) \tag{1}$$

Total economy potential output, *YP*, is taken to equal potential output in the business sector plus actual output in the government sector, *YG*, assuming that the government sector is always producing at potential:

$$YP = YPB + YG \tag{2}$$

The two unobservable variables, *EPB* and *TFPT*, are calculated using a number of supplementary assumptions.[2] A series for actual total factor productivity is calculated based on the production function residual from a simple Cobb-Douglas production without technical progress. This is subsequently smoothed using the Hodrick-Prescott filter to give trend *TFP*. Potential business sector employment depends on the trend labour force, *LFT*, with deductions made for government sector employment, *EG*, and for structural unemployment, *US*:

$$EPB = LFT - EG - US \tag{3}$$

The trend labour force is derived from actual and projected figures for the population of working age combined with the trend participation rates, obtained by Hodrick-Prescott filtering the actual participation rate. Structural unemployment is estimated combining information of wage inflation and actual unemployment. Conceptually, it corresponds to the minimum rate of unemployment which in the short run is associated with non-accelerating wages.[3]

In deriving the output gap estimate for 1994 of 1¾ per cent and the estimate of 1995-96 potential growth of 2¼ per cent, the most important inputs were accordingly:

– Stability of structural unemployment at 4 per cent.
– Trend labour force growth of ¾ per cent.

- Growth of *TFPT* of ³/₄ per cent.
- For government employment and output, actually projected values were used.
- The projection for business fixed investment corresponds to growth of the capital stock of approximately 3³/₄ per cent.

The cyclically-adjusted budget balance

The calculation of cyclically-adjusted budget balances takes the calculated output gap as an input. Various tax items and current, non-interest expenditure are adjusted based on the relative size of the output gap and a set of corresponding elasticities. The individual items and the associated semi-elasticity with respect to the output gap are as follows:[4]

- Corporate tax (2.5).
- Income tax (1.2).
- Social security contributions (0.5).
- Indirect taxes (1.0).
- Government current, non-interest expenditure (–0.1).

Weighting these elasticities according to the shares of the corresponding revenue and expenditure components in GDP gives an indicator of the overall sensitivity of the budget balance to cyclical fluctuations. These overall sensitivities, which measure the change in the budget balance as a share of GDP arising from a 1 percentage point change in the output gap, are plotted in Diagram A1 against the share of government non-interest revenue in GDP in 1993. As can be seen, the cross-country pattern of budget sensitivities broadly follows the size of government revenue, *i.e.* there is an upward-sloping pattern in the Diagram. However, the effects of cross-country differences in elasticities and in the relative shares of various tax components are also of importance as revealed by the fluctuations around the general upward slope. Austria having a share of government revenue close to the average in the OECD, also has a budget sensitivity (0.49) close to the (unweighted) OECD average (0.50).

Government deficit and debt scenarios

Diagram 12 in Part II of the main text employs a simple debt accounting framework to analyse the medium-term budgetary outlook and the requirements for budgetary retrenchment under various assumptions. The framework can be represented by the following set of equations:

$$pdef = pdef(-1) - a*(g - gpot) - disc \tag{4}$$

$$def = pdef + debt(-1)*(i + p)/(1 + p + g) \tag{5}$$

$$debt = def + debt(-1)/(1 + g + p) \tag{6}$$

The first equation specifies the primary deficit, *pdef*, as reflecting its own lagged level, a cyclical change component depending on the difference between actual and

Diagram A1. **GOVERNMENT REVENUE AND THE CYCLICAL SENSITIVITY
OF THE BUDGET BALANCE**

Per cent of GDP

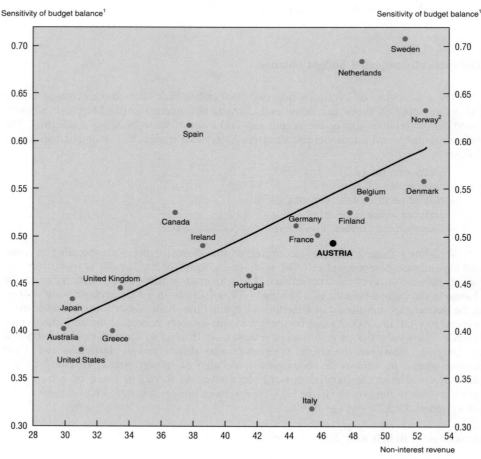

Sensitivity of budget balance[1]

Non-interest revenue

1. Change in the budget balance as a percentage of GDP arising from a 1 percentage point change in the output gap.
2. Refers to the mainland economy of Norway.
Source: OECD.

potential growth, g and $gpot$ respectively, and the discretionary budget improvement, $disc$. Equations (5) and (6) specify, respectively, the deficit and debt dynamics, taking into account the real interest rate, i, inflation, p, and GDP growth. All variables which are not inherently in rate form are measured relative to GDP.

Notes

1. Other procedures are described in Giorno *et al.* (1995) which also contains a more detailed description of the calculation of potential.
2. The construction of capital stock data is described in Keese *et al.* (1991).
3. The procedure is described in Elmeskov and Macfarlan (1994).
4. For the derivation of the tax elasticities, see Giorno *et al.* (1995).

Bibliography

Elmeskov, J. and M. Macfarlan (1994), "Unemployment Persistence", *OECD Economic Studies*, 21.

Giorno, C., P. Richardson, D. Roseveare and P. van den Noord (1995), "Estimating Potential Output, Output Gaps and Structural Budget Balances", *OECD Economics Department Working Papers*, 152.

Keese, M., G. Salou and P. Richardson (1991), "The Measurement of Output and Factors of Production for the Business Sector in OECD Countries", *OECD Economics Department Working Paper*, 99.

Annex II

Supporting material to Part IV

Table A1. **Structural characteristics of market services**

	Banking	Insurance	Road transport	Air transport	Telecom-munications	Construction	Consulting	Trade	Tourism
GDP share, per cent (1991)	5.5	1.6	1.6	0.4	2.5	7.6	0.1	13.4	2.6
Average productivity growth, per cent (1983/88)	1.5	0.2	0.8	7.2	3.6	1.0	..	1.3	-1.5
Average inflation rate, per cent (1980/91)	3.8	5.3	4.2	2.1	2.7	4.4	..	2.2	5.5
Concentration (1991)[1]	52.8	69.3-90.4[2]	L	H	H	22.3	32.0[3]	11.2[3]	25.0
Foreign influence (1992)[4]	12.3	29.4-69.1[2]	L	L	L	20.1	5-6	21.1	L
Economies of scale	L	M	L	M	H	M	L	M	M
Economies of scope	M	M	M	M	H	M	M	M	M
Product differentiation	M	H	L	M	M	M	M	M	H
Nearness to customers	M	M	M	H	M	H	M	M	H
Regulation									
Earlier	SR	SR	SR	SR	SR	SR	SR	SR	PL
Now	FL	FL	SR	PL	PL	PL	PL	PL	FL
Competition intensity									
Now	M	L	H	L	L	M	L	L	M
Potential	H	H	H	M	M	H	M	H	H
Market structure	OC	OC	PC	OC	RM	PC	MC	MC	MC

Note: Qualitative indicators: L = low; H = high; SR = strict regulation; PL = partial liberalisation; FL = full liberalisation; MC = monopolistic competition; OC = oligopolistic competition; PC = perfect competition; RM = regulated monopoly.

1. Where number is given, share of eight largest firms in per cent of total turnover.
2. Lower number refers to life insurance sector; higher to reinsurance (non-life insurance lies in between).
3. In 1988.
4. Where number is given, share of foreign capital.
Source: Breuss (1994).

Table A2. Largest industrial enterprises of Austria

1987

Firm's name	Branch	Total sales in Sch billion	Total employment	Ownership [1]
VOEST-Alpine	Steel	56.7	59 005	S
ÖMV	Oil	47.6	9 270	S [2]
Siemens Austria	Electrical engineering	17.2	15 574	FM
Philips Austria	Electrical engineering	15.2	9 800	FM
Steyr-Daimler-Puch	Car	13.2	12 487	S/B
Chemie Holding	Chemicals	10.9	6 059	S
Constantia Holding	Paper, woodprocessing	10.9	6 100	P
General Motors Austria	Car	9.3	2 600	FM
Schäardinger	Food	8.8	1 527	P
AMAG	Aluminium	7.9	5 103	S
Elin	Electrical engineering	7.9	8 120	S
Unilever Austria	Food	6.9	3 700	FM
Hoechst Austria	Chemicals	6.5	2 090	FM
Bau Holding	Construction	6.5	5 051	S/B
Leykam	Paper	5.8	2 825	S/B
Porr	Construction	5.2	3 601	S/B
Swarovski	Glass	5.1	4 877	P
Veitscher Magnesit	Stone	5.0	3 096	FM
Danubia	Chemicals	4.8	808	S
Lenzing	Chemicals	4.7	3 894	S/B

1. Ownership: S = state-owned (directly); S/B = state-owned through nationalised banks; FM = foreign multinational; P = private Austrian.
2. In 1994, 20 per cent of the State's holdings in ÖMV were sold to the private sector under the government's privatisation programme, and there are plans to sell another 25 per cent.
Source: F. Schneider (1991).

Table A3. Capitalisation of companies listed on the Vienna Stock Exchange by industry

As at 31st December 1993

	Capitalisation	
	Sch million	Per cent
Banks	83 575.0	25.3
Insurance companies	53 173.4	16.1
Construction industry	22 036.9	6.7
Construction materials	25 530.3	7.7
Breweries	15 006.1	4.6
Chemicals	6 512.3	2.0
Energy	55 488.5	16.8
Mining	7 316.4	2.2
Technical sector	17 222.0	5.2
Foodstuffs	6 646.1	2.0
Paper	8 415.4	2.6
Retail/services	2 866.9	0.9
Textiles	1 034.2	0.3
Conglomerates	5 362.9	1.6
Real estate	10 358.5	3.1
Others	9 457.8	2.9
Total	330 002.7	100.0

Source: Austrian National Bank (1993).

Table A4. **Regional structure of Austrian foreign trade from 1920 to 1992**

Shares in per cent

	Exports				Imports			
	1920	1970	1988	1992	1920	1970	1988	1992
Germany[1]	17.0	24.3	36.5	39.8	36.6	42.0	45.0	42.9
Italy	27.8	9.7	10.4	8.8	3.6	6.5	8.9	8.6
Switzerland	7.5	10.4	7.2	5.9	1.1	7.4	4.4	4.0
France	1.4	2.2	4.6	4.4	0.0	3.5	3.9	4.4
United Kingdom	0.4	6.1	4.7	3.6	0.3	6.8	2.5	2.7
United States	1.5	4.1	3.5	2.6	4.8	3.4	3.4	3.9
Monarchy successor states	42.3	12.8	6.1	9.65	0.2	7.4	4.8	5.7
Czechoslovakia (former)	24.8	2.2	1.2	2.83	7.6	1.9	1.3	1.9
Hungary	8.1	2.8	1.8	3.2	3.2	1.7	1.4	2.0
Poland[2]	3.9	1.6	1.0	1.5	5.7	1.6	0.9	0.8
Yugoslavia (former)[2]	3.7	4.6	2.0	1.8	3.5	1.4	1.0	0.8
Romania[2]	1.8	1.6	0.1	0.3	0.2	0.8	0.2	0.2
USSR (CIS)		2.9	2.9	1.6		2.2	1.9	1.4
Bulgaria		0.9	0.6	0.3		0.3	0.1	0.1
Other countries	2.1	26.6	23.5	23.4	3.4	20.5	25.1	26.3
Total	100.0	100.0	100.0	100.0	100.0	100.0	100.0	100.0

1. The figures for 1970 and 1988 include the GDR.
2. Only partly "successor states" of the Monarchy.
Source: Mayerhofer (1992)

Table A5. Telecommunications in selected countries

1992

	Number of enterprises	Moved off-budget	Head company privatised	Market form
Austria	2 [1,2]	No	No	M
Belgium	1	1990	No	M
Denmark	1 + 4 [2]	1987	1992	M
Finland	1 + 8 [2]	1987	No	C
France	1	1986/1990	No	M
Germany	1	1989	No	M
Iceland	1	No	No	M
Italy	5 [2]	–	–	M
Japan	n [3]	1952	1985	C
Netherlands	2	1989	No	D
Norway	1	1990	No	M
Spain	1	1924	1924	M
Sweden	2 + n	Since beginning	No	C
Switzerland	1	1992	No	M
United Kingdom	3 + n	1968/1981	1984	C
United States	n [3]	Since beginning	Since beginning	C

Note: M = monopoly; D = duopoly; C = open competition; n = many.
1. PTV and Radio Austria Communications.
2. Geographically or functionally divided enterprises.
3. Various local, national and international enterprises.
Source: Breuss (1994); OECD (1995).

Table A6. Trade margins, costs and earnings by enterprise size

1983; in per cent of turnover

Annual turnover in Sch 1 000	Wholesale			Retail		
	Trade margins	Costs	Earnings	Trade margins	Costs	Earnings
1 to 250	81.6	68.8	12.8	46.6	38.5	8.1
251 to 500	77.9	58.1	19.8	42.2	31.6	10.6
501 to 1 000	68.8	49.0	19.8	36.8	25.3	11.5
1 001 to 5 000	43.2	34.2	9.0	29.5	21.2	8.3
5 001 to 10 000	33.8	27.1	6.7	27.4	20.3	7.1
10 001 to 50 000	29.2	23.9	5.3	28.9	23.0	5.9
50 001 to 100 000	26.2	22.4	3.8	27.9	22.6	5.3
100 001 and above	14.7	12.1	2.6	27.1	21.7	5.4

Source: Breuss (1994).

Table A7. **Import structure and tariff regime**
1993

	Imports			Tariff regime		
	Value Sch billion	Share in total	Share in group	Before EU entry	In the EU	Change
		Per cent				
Industrial goods	**528.4**	**93.4**	**100.0**			
EU and EFTA	394.8	69.8	74.7	Free	Free	No
Near-east Europe [1]	24.2	4.3	4.6	Free [2]	Free	No
Other east Europe	12.2	2.2	2.3	−50% [3]	Free [4]	Yes
Developing countries	42.8	7.6	8.1	−50% [3]	Free [4]	Yes
Other countries	54.4	9.6	10.3	Yes	Yes	Yes [5]
Agricultural goods	**37.1**	**6.6**	**100.0**			
EU 12	20.6	3.6	55.5	Yes	Free	Yes
EFTA	0.9	0.2	2.4	Yes	Free	Yes
Other countries	15.6	2.8	42.0	Yes	Yes	Yes [6]
Total goods	**565.5**	**100.0**	..			
Memorandum item:						
Average tariff rate [7]				8.3	3.3	

1. Central-east Europe plus Bulgaria plus Romania.
2. Excepting for some ''sensitive'' products.
3. GSP tariff reductions of 50 per cent from basic rate.
4. Quotas exist, however.
5. Lowering of average tariff rate.
6. Change in the system.
7. For industrial goods, weighted, after the Uruguay Round.
Source: Stankovsky (1994).

Annex III

Industrial classifications

A. Classification according to production process and market structure (OECD STAN classification):

Economies of scale:

2 – Food, beverages and tobacco
5 – Paper products and printing
7 – Chemicals
8 – Drugs and medicine
9 – Petroleum products
10 – Rubber and plastic
13 – Iron and steel
14 – Non-ferrous metals
21 – Shipbuilding and repair
22 – Motor vehicles
23 – Aircraft
24 – Other transport equipment

Differentiated market (economies of scope):

2 – Food, beverages and tobacco
7 – Chemicals
8 – Drugs and medicines
16 – Metal products
17 – Non-electrical machinery
18 – Office and computing machinery
19 – Electrical machines
20 – Radio, television, communications
22 – Motor vehicles
23 – Aircraft
24 – Other transport equipment
25 – Professional goods

B. Classification based on primary factors affecting competitiveness (ISIC Rev. 2 classification):

Resource-intensive industries

  31 – Manufacturing of food, beverages and tobacco
 323 – Manufacturing of leather, except footwear and wearing apparel
 331 – Manufacturing of wood, wood and cork products, except furniture
3411 – Manufacturing of pulp, paper and paperboard
 353 – Petroleum refineries
 354 – Miscellaneous products of petroleum and coal
 369 – Other non-metallic mineral products
 372 – Non-ferrous metal basic industries

Labour-intensive industries

321/322/324 – Textile, wearing apparel and footwear industries
       332 – Manufacture of furniture and fixtures, except primarily metal
 380/381 – Metal scrap from manufactures of fabricated metal products and fabricated metal products, excluding machinery and equipment
        39 – Other manufacturing industries

Scale-intensive industries

  34 – Manufacture of paper, paper products, printing, publishing, except 3411
 351 – Manufacture of industrial chemicals
 355 – Rubber products
 356 – Plastic products not elsewhere classified
361/362 – Manufacture of pottery, china, earthenware, glass and glass products
 371 – Iron and steel basic industries
 384 – Transport equipment, excluding 3845

Differentiated goods

3821 – Engines and turbines
3822 – Agricultural machinery and equipment
3823 – Metal and woodworking machinery
3824 – Special industrial machinery and equipment, excluding 3823
 383 – Electrical machinery, apparatus, appliances and supplies
3852/3 – Photographic and optical goods, watches and clocks

Science-based industries

352 – Manufacture of other chemical products
3825 – Office, computing and accounting machinery
3851 – Professional, scientific, measuring and controlling equipment
3845 – Aircraft

Chronology of main economic events

1994

January

The EEA comes into being on 4 January.

February

The negotiations for EU entry are formally opened. Twenty-one out of twenty-nine chapters of the agreement have already been largely covered in the EEA agreement. Main points of negotiation remaining are: Chapter 4, free capital movements (second residence question); Chapter 5, transportation policy (transit traffic); Chapter 15, agriculture; Chapter 27, financial and budgetary conditions.

The Austrian National Bank lowers the discount and Lombard rates by $1/4$ percentage point each, to 5 and 6 per cent respectively.

March

Austria successfully concludes its EU accession negotiations. Main points are as follows:

- *Free capital movements:* the legal restrictions on purchases of second residences can be maintained by Austria for a transition period of five years. Thus, national, regional, or local rules relating to environmental planning or environmental protection could be encountered. However, these will not discriminate against citizens of other EU countries as they also apply to Austrian citizens.
- *Transportation policy:* the 1992 transport agreement between Austria and the EU sought to reduce nitrous oxide emissions by heavy vehicles between 1991 and 2003 by 60 per cent. To this end the eco-point system was introduced. The new agreement incorporates three treaty phases of three years each. Until 1 January 1998 the eco-point system will be in force and reviewed; unless all parties agree

133

to lift the agreement, it will as of this date be renewed for another three years. Before the end of that three-year period, the European environmental agency will be charged with reviewing whether the goal of the 60 per cent reduction of NO has been reached. If so, the transport agreement will be abolished; otherwise, the treaty remains in force for a third three-year term. Austria in turn commits itself to strengthen railroad capacity and infrastructure. By 31 October 1994 Austria, Germany and Italy should decide about the construction of the Brenner mountain tunnel; the possibility for financing out of the EU budget, in the framework of the union programme for trans-European networks, will be allowed for this purpose.

– *Agriculture:* Austria must take over the common agricultural policy; borders to trade in agricultural goods will also be eliminated. Austria is entitled to the following national quotas and reference quantities – sugar: 390 410 tonnes; milk: 2 752 000 tonnes; cattle: 423 400 heads; cows: 325 000 heads; sheep: 205 651 heads; tobacco 600 tonnes. In the framework of the agricultural structural policy, the delimitation and granting of aids for mountain areas and other disadvantaged areas will be allowed; first review is envisaged after five years. Investment support for related branches will also be forthcoming. The EU has accepted an environmental programme presented by Austria and will contribute Sch 2.4 billion per year to its financing. Also, agricultural concerns will be taken into account in the framework of regional aids. For the transition of agriculture into the internal market, the EU-imposed "internal market model" will apply: the production price will fall to the EU level upon entry with the EU and the agricultural market will be immediately opened. Over four years, "degressive equalisation payments" are foreseen for the agricultural sector; these will be co-financed by the EU. For sensitive agricultural goods and processed goods, a protection clause will be in effect for five years, which will serve to counteract severe market disturbances.

– *Financial and budgetary rules:* Austria shares in the common assets and thus participates in the financing of the common budget in the amount of Sch 29 billion per year. In 1995, with payments from the EU to Austria of around Sch 17 billion, a net contribution to the EU of around 12 billion is foreseen.

April

The Austrian National Bank lowers the discount and Lombard rates each by $1/4$ percentage point to $4^3/4$ and $5^3/4$ per cent, respectively.

May

New collective wage agreements come into effect: workers in the tourist industry receive a 3.1 per cent collective wages increase; in the construction industry, 3.6 to 3.7 per cent collective wage increase; in the chemical industry, 3.8 per cent collective wage and 2.8 per cent Ist-wage (effective) but Sch 550 at a minimum; in the textile industry, a minimum wage increase of Sch 2 per hour and an Ist-wage increase of Sch 2.2 per hour, the latter amounts to about a 2.5 per cent increase.

The National Bank reduces the discount and Lombard rates by ¼ percentage points each to 4½ and 5½ per cent respectively.

June

In a popular referendum on EU membership, the outcome is 66.6 per cent in favour of membership with an 82.4 per cent turnout.

July

With the minimum reserve announcements of January, February, and March 1994, the Austrian National Bank has carried out the legal adaptation to the 1 January *Bank Act*. For purposes of the minimum reserve requirement, bearer instruments will be treated as securities, and registered securities will be treated as bank deposits. Savings and loan (building society) deposits remain free of minimum reserve requirements, but obligations arising out of registered bonds will be subject to such requirements.

The *Labour Market Service Law* transfers labour market management from the central government to the Labour Market Service (AMS), a service enterprise with its own legal status. Labour market placement by private agencies is allowed. The rules for financing of the AMS are established in the *Labour Market Policy Financing Law*. The personnel and material expenses of the AMS will be reimbursed by the central government in a lump sum; as to support payments, the AMS acts as an official agency directly in the name of and on the account of the central government.

The *Environmental Impact Review Law* comes into effect. Project initiators must submit their investment plans to the regional environmental review authority for an environmental impact study. Projects which are too small to undergo examination by the environmental authority, but which may be expected to impact on the environment, have to undergo a citizens' review process.

The 1994 amendment to the *Market Regulation Law* comes into effect: the grain and fertilizer charges are eliminated.

September

Bankruptcy proceedings for the largest Austrian ski factory, Atomic, are opened. With net liabilities of around Sch 1.8 billion, this is the largest domestic insolvency so far this year and ranks among the top twelve in modern history.

October

National parliamentary elections give 34.9 per cent of the vote to the SPÖ (Social Democrats), 27.7 per cent to the ÖVP (People's Party), 22.5 per cent of the FPÖ (Freedom Party), 7.3 per cent to the Greens, and 6 per cent to the Liberal Forum.

November

Wages and salaries in the metal-working and electrical engineering industries are raised by 3½ per cent. The collectively-agreed minimum wage is raised by 3.8 per cent, on top of which is granted a one-time "conjuncture-premium" of Sch 2 000.

President Klestil and Chancellor Vranitzky sign the ratification document for EU-entry by Austria.

A working agreement between the Social Democratic Party and the People's Party forms the basis for the coalition government for the 19th legislative period. The avowed central economic goal of the coalition is budget consolidation towards attainment of the Maastricht criteria for entry into the Economic and Monetary Union. Thus, within this legislative period, the general government deficit is to be reduced to below 3 per cent of GDP.

December

At the European Monetary Institute in Frankfurt, the Austrian National Bank signs the agreements establishing the conditions for entry by Austria into the European Monetary System. Thus, entry into the EMS can be achieved simultaneously with entry into the EU. The exchange policy of Austria, characterised by a tight linking of the Schilling to the Deutschmark, will be continued.

1995

January

Austria enters the EU.

Salaries in the trade sector are raised by 3.6 per cent, while the minimum salary is raised by 4.6 per cent. In the public sector, salaries are raised by 2.9 per cent.

STATISTICAL ANNEX AND STRUCTURAL INDICATORS

Table A. Gross domestic product
Sch billion

	Current prices					1983 prices				
	1989	1990	1991	1992	1993	1989	1990	1991	1992	1993
Expenditure										
Private consumption	935.3	999.2	1 064.0	1 127.1	1 168.3	799.8	828.6	853.0	869.6	871.2
Public consumption	302.9	319.9	349.6	377.1	405.6	239.2	242.1	249.5	255.5	263.2
Gross domestic fixed capital formation	405.8	442.4	488.4	511.1	511.3	347.9	367.8	391.1	396.1	387.9
Construction[1]	229.0	250.5	279.9	303.5	319.7	195.1	206.4	219.1	230.0	235.0
Machinery and equipment[1]	176.7	191.9	208.5	207.6	191.6	152.8	161.5	172.0	166.1	153.0
Change of stocks, incl. statistical errors	14.1	17.5	8.8	4.2	8.7	10.6	17.3	7.8	6.8	7.7
Exports of goods and services	664.3	724.3	770.4	803.4	803.4	610.6	659.9	699.2	718.7	711.7
Less: Imports of goods and services	649.4	702.0	753.0	776.8	779.4	621.8	670.4	712.6	731.3	727.2
Gross domestic product at market prices	1 672.9	1 801.3	1 928.3	2 046.1	2 117.8	1 386.4	1 445.3	1 487.9	1 515.4	1 514.5
Origin by sector										
Agriculture, forestry and fishing	52.3	56.7	53.0	50.1	48.4	46.1	48.1	44.9	43.6	44.2
Manufacturing and mining	437.6	469.3	496.1	507.0	500.2	390.8	410.2	422.3	421.7	406.6
Construction	113.5	124.3	140.0	153.3	161.8	96.0	99.1	105.0	110.6	112.9
Other	1 069.5	1 151.0	1 239.2	1 335.7	1 407.5	853.5	887.9	915.7	939.5	950.7

	Current prices					Current prices, percentage distribution				
	1989	1990	1991	1992	1993	1989	1990	1991	1992	1993
Distribution of net national income										
Compensation of employees	874.5	940.1	1 020.8	1 095.7	1 142.4	71.3	70.7	71.7	72.1	73.1
Net income from property and entrepreneurship and savings of corporations	372.2	416.9	440.9	457.7	464.8	30.3	31.4	31.0	30.1	29.7
Direct taxes on corporations	35.7	37.9	42.8	50.8	50.0	2.9	2.8	3.0	3.3	3.2
Government income from property and entrepreneurship	33.3	38.1	40.8	45.7	42.8	2.7	2.9	2.9	3.0	2.7
Less: Interest on public and consumer debt	89.1	103.3	121.0	130.7	136.4	7.3	7.8	8.5	8.6	8.7
Net national income	1 226.6	1 329.6	1 424.3	1 519.2	1 563.6	100.0	100.0	100.0	100.0	100.0

1. Excluding VAT.
Source: Österreichisches Statistisches Zentralamt, and Österreichisches Institut für Wirtschaftsforschung.

Table B. **General government income and expenditure**

Sch. billion

	1985	1986	1987	1988	1989	1990	1991	1992	1993
Operating surplus and property income receivable	26.2	25.9	29.4	30.7	33.3	38.1	40.8	45.7	42.8
Casualty insurance claims receivable	0.2	0.3	0.3	0.3	0.4	0.4	0.4	0.4	0.7
Indirect taxes	225.9	234.0	245.2	254.9	271.4	287.9	305.8	325.8	338.6
Direct taxes	193.7	203.8	203.4	214.5	214.5	238.9	267.1	297.7	304.9
Compulsory fees, fines and penalties	3.8	3.9	3.9	4.1	4.4	4.9	5.1	5.1	5.1
Social security contributions	167.8	176.0	183.3	191.8	204.3	220.6	238.9	262.3	279.8
Unfunded employee welfare contributions imputed	35.3	37.6	39.6	41.1	43.4	46.0	49.8	53.2	56.3
Current transfers n.e.c. received from the rest of the world	0.7	0.7	0.7	0.6	0.6	0.7	0.9	0.8	0.8
Current receipts	653.6	682.2	705.8	738.0	772.3	837.5	908.8	991.0	1 029.0
Final consumption expenditure	255.0	270.7	280.4	288.4	302.9	319.9	349.6	377.1	405.6
Property income payable	47.8	51.9	58.4	61.8	66.4	73.1	82.1	87.9	93.0
Net casualty insurance premiums payable	0.2	0.3	0.3	0.3	0.4	0.4	0.4	0.4	0.4
Subsidies	39.2	46.0	47.4	45.1	45.1	47.9	56.4	61.2	63.5
Social security benefits and social assistance grants	142.3	151.1	161.5	167.8	176.4	188.7	199.9	212.3	227.9
Current transfers to private non-profit institutions serving household	76.3	80.4	87.0	85.2	86.4	94.1	103.7	117.3	133.2
Unfunded employee welfare benefits	56.2	59.9	63.4	66.0	70.1	74.5	80.8	86.0	91.7
Current transfers n.e.c. paid to the rest of the world	3.6	3.8	3.9	4.3	4.7	5.5	6.5	8.0	9.1
Current disbursements	620.6	664.1	702.3	718.9	752.4	804.1	879.4	950.2	1 024.4
Saving	33.0	18.1	3.5	19.1	19.9	33.4	29.4	40.8	4.6
Consumption of fixed capital	10.7	11.3	11.6	11.8	12.2	12.8	13.5	13.8	14.5
Capital transfers received net, from:	-27.1	-27.5	-26.8	-27.3	-23.1	-27.0	-26.5	-28.9	-37.2
Other resident sectors	-27.1	-27.5	-26.8	-27.3	-23.0	-26.9	-26.3	-28.7	-36.8
The rest of the world	0.0	0.0	0.0	0.0	-0.1	-0.1	-0.2	-0.2	-0.4
Finance of gross accumulation	16.6	1.9	-11.7	3.6	9.0	19.2	16.4	25.7	-18.1
Gross capital formation	48.0	52.1	50.7	50.7	55.2	57.3	62.6	67.3	65.9
Purchases of land, net	1.8	2.2	0.7	0.6	0.6	0.7	0.9	0.0	3.1
Net lending	-33.2	-52.4	-63.1	-47.7	-46.8	-38.8	-47.1	-41.6	-87.1

Source: Bundesministerium für Finanzen.

Table C. **Output, employment and productivity in industry**

	1983	1984	1985	1986	1987	1988	1989	1990	1991	1992	1993
Output in industry, 1990 = 100											
Total industry	75.0	78.9	82.5	83.4	84.2	87.9	93.1	100.0	101.6	100.5	98.5
Investment goods	69.4	71.5	80.1	83.1	77.0	81.1	86.5	100.0	105.3	102.6	97.4
Consumer goods	82.0	86.5	88.8	89.2	87.9	87.8	93.4	100.0	102.2	100.1	99.2
Intermediate goods	68.1	76.8	79.2	79.3	80.7	87.8	93.6	100.0	100.5	100.4	97.5
Manufacturing goods	80.5	85.4	88.3	82.1	81.0	86.4	92.1	100.0	102.0	101.2	98.5
Employment, thousands[1]	565.1	561.4	562.4	558.8	543.6	532.6	536.3	544.8	538.9	520.5	487.4
Monthly hours worked[2]	144.3	145.2	144.9	142.1	139.9	141.0	139.9	139.5	138.2	138.2	137.9
Wages and productivity											
Gross hourly earnings for wage earners (sch.)	86.8	90.0	95.1	99.3	104.3	107.8	112.6	120.7	127.9	135.3	142.0
Gross monthly earnings, employees (sch.)	17 739.9	18 625.9	19 755.4	20 713.3	21 504.5	22 338.9	23 389.5	25 143.5	26 592.8	28 207.7	29 613.2
Output per employee (1990 = 100)	70.6	75.5	78.5	79.9	81.5	88.2	93.3	100.0	102.5	105.1	108.7

1. Including administrative personnel.
2. Mining and manufacturing.
Source: Österreichisches Institut für Wirtschaftsforschung, and Österreichisches Statistiches Zentralamt.

Table D. **Retail sales and prices**
(1990 = 100)

	1983	1984	1985	1986	1987	1988	1989	1990	1991	1992	1993
Retail sales	77.7	78.3	82.0	82.6	85.0	89.2	93.5	100.0	107.5	111.6	112.0
of which: durables	67.5	62.4	69.0	74.5	78.0	86.3	92.8	100.0	108.0	112.5	112.0
Prices											
Consumer prices											
Total	82.4	87.0	89.8	91.3	92.6	94.4	96.8	100.0	103.3	107.5	111.4
Food	85.4	90.3	92.3	94.5	95.2	95.9	97.1	100.0	104.1	108.2	111.3
Rent	76.6	82.0	86.4	89.1	91.1	93.3	96.1	100.0	105.0	111.0	116.8
Other goods and services	82.2	86.7	89.7	90.6	92.0	94.1	96.8	100.0	102.9	106.9	110.8
Wholesale prices											
Total	96.9	100.5	103.2	97.7	95.8	95.5	97.2	100.0	100.9	100.6	100.2
Agricultural goods	94.1	97.9	99.9	90.8	94.4	93.2	93.1	100.0	101.6	91.3	88.7
Food	96.3	101.6	105.1	105.2	102.3	101.5	100.8	100.0	102.6	107.8	108.8
Cost of construction (residential)	80.9	83.8	85.3	86.7	90.0	92.8	96.1	100.0	105.9	110.7	114.2

Source: Österreichisches Statistisches Zentralamt, and Österreichisches Institut für Wirtschaftsforschung.

Table E. **Money and banking**[1]

End of period

Sch billion

	1984	1985	1986	1987	1988	1989	1990	1991	1992	1993
Interest rates (per cent)										
Discount rate	4.50	4.00	4.00	3.00	4.00	6.50	6.50	8.00	8.00	5.25
Average bond yield[2]	7.98	7.74	7.3	6.86	6.58	7.06	8.72	8.69	8.39	6.74
Money circulation and external reserves										
Notes and coins in circulation	93.7	94.5	98.1	102.9	108.4	117.8	124.7	133.4	141.2	149.8
Sight liabilities of the Central Bank	48.8	46.6	53.0	43.6	39.6	51.1	44.3	38.8	48.9	55.6
Gross external reserves of the Central Bank	118.6	110.5	115.0	114.9	123.4	132.8	130.3	140.1	167.4	202.4
of which: Gold	39.4	39.4	39.5	39.5	39.5	38.6	38.1	37.4	37.2	34.7
Credit institutions										
Credits to domestic non-banks	1 114.4	1 211.6	1 333.6	1 438.2	1 579.4	1 688.4	1 846.2	1 994.2	2 129.7	2 202.1
Deposits from domestic non-banks	989.4	1 058.2	1 170.7	1 259.2	1 312.3	1 404.3	1 503.8	1 613.9	1 680.3	1 751.9
Sight	102.7	107.5	113.5	129.1	142.2	146.5	155.9	170.8	180.9	207.2
Time[3]	113.9	124.1	162.8	176.3	174.4	198.8	185.8	172.4	136.9	118.0
Savings	772.8	826.6	894.4	953.7	995.7	1 059.0	1 162.1	1 270.7	1 362.5	1 426.7
Holdings of domestic Treasury bills	46.2	41.0	41.0	51.2	46.9	44.9	53.7	60.4	56.3	67.0
Holdings of other domestic securities	228.2	233.1	249.9	287.0	319.5	345.7	356.1	365.0	342.4	376.2
Foreign assets	633.5	695.9	737.6	751.7	816.9	842.0	843.9	846.8	915.9	1 012.4
Foreign liabilities	676.7	724.6	772.4	794.7	883.8	933.0	937.8	962.0	1 048.8	1 088.4

1. Totals may not add due to rounding.
2. Average effective yields on circulating issues.
3. Including funded borrowing of banks.

Source: Österreichische Nationalbank, and Österreichische Länderbank.

Table F. **The Federal budget**

National accounts basis

Sch billion

	Outturn								
	1985	1986	1987	1988	1989	1990	1991	1992	1993
1. Current revenue	330.3	343.7	354.8	389.2	404.6	437.5	473.2	518.9	526.3
Direct taxes of households	102.1	107.6	105.1	129.9	124.8	140.1	154.1	167.1	169.9
Indirect taxes	157.9	164.0	173.1	178.8	190.1	201.2	213.2	229.0	236.1
Corporate taxes	20.2	20.4	19.9	21.0	25.1	26.3	30.5	38.0	36.8
Income from property and entrepreneurship	18.9	18.8	22.4	23.1	24.9	27.6	29.1	33.5	30.6
Current transfers from abroad	0.4	0.3	0.3	0.3	0.2	0.3	0.4	0.2	0.2
Other	30.8	32.6	34.0	36.1	39.5	42.0	45.9	51.1	52.7
2. Current expenditure	340.5	367.5	392.2	403.6	414.7	441.3	488.9	520.1	570.6
Goods and services	95.6	101.2	102.0	104.3	109.0	113.7	122.8	130.1	138.9
Subsidies	30.0	36.4	37.5	34.7	34.1	35.2	42.9	44.6	49.4
Public debt	38.4	42.7	49.4	53.1	58.0	64.3	73.1	78.7	84.0
Transfers to abroad	1.0	1.0	1.0	1.1	1.2	1.6	2.0	2.1	2.7
Transfers to public authorities	82.0	87.6	96.3	105.5	105.5	111.0	121.4	125.4	140.0
Transfers to private households	59.3	62.3	67.6	65.0	64.5	70.5	77.5	87.2	99.9
Other	34.2	36.3	38.4	39.9	42.4	45.0	49.2	52.0	55.7
3. Net public savings (1-2)	−10.2	−23.8	−37.4	−14.4	−10.1	−3.8	−15.8	−1.2	−44.3
4. Depreciation	2.4	2.6	2.6	2.7	2.8	2.9	3.1	3.1	3.3
5. Gross savings (3 + 4)	−7.8	−21.2	−34.8	−11.7	−7.3	−0.9	−12.7	1.9	−41.0
6. Gross asset formation	17.8	18.5	15.5	15.2	15.4	16.0	16.8	15.1	15.8
7. Balance of income-effective transactions (5-6)	−25.6	−39.7	−50.3	−26.9	−22.7	−16.9	−29.7	−13.2	−56.8
8. Capital transfers (net)	23.7	24.4	23.2	39.0	34.8	37.8	40.0	41.5	45.8
9. Financial balance (7-8)	−49.3	−64.1	−73.5	−65.9	−57.5	−54.7	−69.5	−54.7	−102.6

Source: Österreichisches Statistiches Zentralamt.

Table G. **Balance of payments**

Sch million

	1984	1985	1986	1987	1988	1989	1990	1991	1992	1993
Trade balance[1]	-76 784	-67 669	-62 231	-65 697	-70 368	-81 727	-90 168	-112 869	-106 365	-97 738
Exports	324 606	366 544	342 659	342 714	375 541	427 511	466 065	479 029	487 558	467 171
Imports	401 390	434 213	404 890	408 411	445 909	509 238	556 233	591 898	593 923	564 909
Services, net	48 429	49 085	42 007	40 354	45 062	57 750	73 148	77 546	85 900	87 832
Foreign travel, net	48 529	48 853	44 884	41 349	46 726	58 881	64 666	74 842	67 400	61 427
Receipts	101 026	105 186	106 195	112 030	124 617	141 782	152 441	161 178	159 640	157 520
Expenditure	52 497	56 333	61 311	70 681	77 891	82 901	87 775	86 336	92 240	96 093
Investment income, net	-7 030	-5 334	-10 104	-10 856	-11 279	-12 324	-10 976	-17 562	-13 083	-11 533
Other services, net	6 930	5 566	7 227	9 861	9 615	11 193	19 458	20 266	31 583	37 938
Unclassified goods and services	25 625	18 045	24 631	23 633	21 833	27 841	30 681	36 349	30 456	14 377
Transfers, net	-1 206	-1 947	-657	-1 023	-433	-1 681	-26	-206	-11 619	-12 716
Public	-766	-799	-690	-898	-894	-945	-2 138	-2 307	-5 382	-6 831
Private	-440	-1 148	33	-125	461	-736	2 112	2 101	-6 237	-5 885
Current balance	-3 936	-2 486	3 750	-2 733	-3 906	2 183	13 635	820	-1 628	-8 245
Long-term capital, net	-7 096	-3 650	9 928	23 040	6 068	4 450	-10 207	-24 383	7 871	75 318
Basic balance	-11 032	-6 136	13 678	20 307	2 162	6 633	3 428	-23 563	6 243	67 073
Short-term capita, net	14 740	-6 687	6 719	-18 382	7 082	5 165	8 942	24 818	13 182	-34 851
Errors and omissions	-2 080	11 626	-11 944	2 818	-3 161	-232	-12 967	7 955	8 348	-5 612
Balance on official settlements[3]	1 628	-1 197	8 453	4 743	6 083	11 566	-597	9 210	27 773	26 610
Memorandum items										
Changes in reserves arising from allocation of SDRs, monetization of gold and revaluation of reserve currencies	4 706	-9 601	-6 960	-4 834	3 266	-2 736	-3 083	1 144	2 184	7 603
Allocation of SDRs	0	0	0	0	0	0	0	0	0	0
Change in total reserves	6 334	-10 802	1 491	-92	9 351	8 830	-3 723	10 307	29 957	34 206
Conversion factor (Sch per dollar)	20.01	20.69	15.27	12.64	12.34	13.23	11.37	11.67	10.99	11.63

1. Including non monetary gold and adjustments to trade according to foreign trade statistics.
2. Including Central Bank.
3. Excluding allocation of SDRs, monetization of gold and revaluation of reserve currencies.
Source: Österreichische Nationalbank.

Table H. **Merchandise trade by commodity group and area**

Sch billion

	Imports					Exports				
	1989	1990	1991	1992	1993	1989	1990	1991	1992	1993
Total	514.9	558.1	593.0	594.7	565.0	429.6	467.7	480.0	488.0	468.1
By commodity group										
Food, drink, tobacco	26.8	27.7	29.5	29.1	29.2	15.2	15.2	15.2	15.9	15.9
Raw materials	27.8	25.3	25.4	24.6	21.9	23.4	24.4	21.5	19.9	18.4
Mineral fuels, energy	29.3	35.4	35.5	30.5	28.4	5.5	4.7	4.4	5.2	5.2
Chemicals	52.1	55.3	57.7	58.4	58.8	39.8	39.5	42.8	42.1	42.1
Machinery and transport equipment	191.2	211.6	232.1	234.8	213.2	148.0	175.6	184.0	189.7	182.4
Other	187.6	202.9	212.8	217.3	213.5	197.7	208.3	212.1	215.2	204.1
By area										
OECD countries	438.2	474.3	501.6	503.3	472.4	355.6	383.6	390.2	394.3	369.8
EU countries	351.6	383.0	402.0	403.9	378.6	279.8	304.8	316.2	322.6	296.8
Germany	226.8	245.5	255.0	255.2	234.3	153.9	175.1	187.5	194.5	182.0
Italy	46.2	50.5	52.4	51.3	50.9	45.3	45.8	45.0	42.9	36.9
France	22.7	23.4	25.8	26.3	24.8	20.0	22.2	20.9	21.4	20.7
United Kingdom	12.9	14.4	16.0	16.2	15.4	19.3	18.1	17.4	17.5	15.2
EFTA countries[1]	36.6	39.4	40.8	40.6	37.9	45.6	47.3	44.1	42.2	41.5
Switzerland	21.3	23.8	24.8	23.8	23.1	31.1	32.4	30.6	29.0	29.8
United States	18.6	20.2	23.4	23.5	24.9	15.0	15.0	13.6	12.9	15.4
Other OECD countries	31.4	31.6	35.4	35.3	31.0	15.3	16.5	16.2	16.6	16.0
Non-OECD countries										
Eastern Europe[2]	28.9	31.8	35.7	38.5	37.9	33.1	36.5	43.0	47.3	48.9
Africa[3]	11.5	13.8	12.9	11.0	11.3	7.5	7.5	7.7	6.4	6.4
Latin America[3]	5.8	5.0	5.1	4.4	4.2	2.4	2.4	2.8	3.0	3.2
OPEC	9.4	12.0	12.5	11.5	11.9	11.3	12.8	13.8	13.8	12.6
Far and Middle East[3]	23.9	26.5	31.4	32.2	33.8	20.8	24.2	25.8	26.9	28.2
Index, in real terms (1988 = 100)	110.6	122.7	124.3	130.1	128.9	113.4	125.6	132.8	139.2	135.7
Index of average value (1988 = 100)	102.7	100.1	100.3	98.9	95.6	97.5	97.2	94.0	92.1	88.1

1. Including Finland.
2. Excluding ex-Yugoslavia.
3. Including countries belonging to OPEC.
Source: Österreichisches Institut für Wirtschaftsforschung.

Table I. **Labour-market indicators**

	Preceding		1987	1988	1989	1990	1991	1992	1993
	Peak	Trough							
			A. EVOLUTION						
Unemployment rate (surveys)									
Total	1983 = 4.1	1973 = 1.1	3.8	3.6	3.1	3.2	3.5	3.6	4.2
Male	1984 = 3.9	1973 = 0.7	3.6	3.3	2.8	3.0	3.4	3.5	4.0
Women	1983 = 5.1	1973 = 1.7	4.1	4.0	3.6	3.6	3.7	3.8	4.5
Unemployment rate (registered)									
Total	1987 = 5.6	1973 = 1.6	5.6	5.4	5.0	5.4	5.8	6.0	6.8
Male			5.5	5.1	4.6	4.9	5.3	5.7	6.7
Women			5.7	5.6	5.5	6.0	6.5	6.2	6.9
Youth			2.7	2.8	2.4	2.6	2.6	2.5	2.9
Share of long-term unemployment			15.0	12.7	16.7	15.8	19.2	20.9	20.6
Productivity index, 1991 = f00			91.0	94.4	97.0	99.1	100.0	99.6	99.4
Monthly hours of work in industry (wage earners) billions of hours			139.9	141.0	139.9	139.5	138.2	138.2	137.9
			B. STRUCTURAL OR INSTITUTIONAL CHARACTERISTICS						
Participation rates[1]									
Global			67.0	66.9	67.1	67.7	68.4	69.4	: :
Male			81.2	80.3	80.0	80.1	80.5	80.7	: :
Women			53.0	53.7	54.3	55.4	56.3	58.0	
Employment/population between 16 and 64 years[1]			64.4	64.5	65.0	65.5	66.0	66.9	:
Employment by sector									
Agriculture									
– per cent of total			8.7	8.2	7.9	7.9	7.4	7.1	6.9
– per cent change			0.4	-5.4	-1.6	1.2	-4.3	-2.4	-1.9
Industry									
– per cent of total			37.7	37.4	37.0	36.8	36.9	35.6	35.0
– per cent change			0.2	-0.4	-0.2	1.6	2.1	-1.7	-0.8
Services									
– per cent of total			53.7	54.4	55.1	55.3	55.7	57.4	58.1
– per cent change			0.8	1.7	2.3	2.5	2.4	5.1	1.9
Voluntary part-time work			8.0	8.2	9.7	9.9	9.8	10.0	: :
Social insurance as a per cent of compensation			18.3	18.5	18.5	18.4	18.3	17.9	17.2

1. Including the self-employed.
Source: Statistisches Handbuch; Österreichisches Institut fur Wirtschaftsforschung; OECD estimates; OECD, *Labour Force Statistics.*

Table J. **Public sector**

	1970	1980	1990	1992	1993
	BUDGET INDICATORS: GENERAL GOVERNMENT ACCOUNTS (% GDP)				
Current receipts	39.7	46.4	46.5	48.4	48.6
Non-interest expenditure	37.4	45.6	44.6	46.2	48.3
Primary budget balance	2.3	0.8	1.9	2.3	0.3
Gross interest	1.1	2.5	4.1	4.3	4.4
General government budget balance	1.2	−1.7	−2.1	−2.0	−4.1
Of which: Federal government	0.2	−2.6	−3.1	−2.7	−4.9
	THE STRUCTURE OF EXPENDITURE (% GDP)				
Government expenditure					
Transfers	4.0	5.9	5.6	6.1	6.7
Subsidies	1.7	3.0	2.7	3.0	3.0
General expenditure	14.7	18.0	17.8	18.4	19.2
Education	2.9	3.9	4.0	4.1	..
Health	3.2	4.4	4.6	4.9	..
Social security and welfare	2.6	3.3	3.2	3.4	..

	TAX RATES	
	Prior to Tax Reform of 1989	Under the Tax Reform of 1989
Personal income tax		
Top rate	62	50
Lower rate	21	10
Average tax rate	12.7	11.5
Social security tax rate[1]		
Blue-collar workers	38.6	38.6
White-collar workers	34.5	34.5
Basic VAT rate	20	20
Corporation tax rate		
Top rate	55	30
Lower rate	30	30

1. The sum of employees' and employers' contributions to health, accident, pension and unemployment insurance.
Source: OECD, *National Accounts*; Ministry of Finance.

Table K. **Production structure and performance indicators**

A. Production structure (1985 prices)

	GDP share (per cent of total)					Employment share (per cent of total)				
	1980	1989	1990	1991	1992	1980	1989	1990	1991	1992
Tradeables										
Agriculture	4.2	3.8	3.8	3.4	3.3	1.7	1.3	1.2	1.2	1.2
Mining and quarrying	0.7	0.4	0.4	0.4	0.3	0.6	0.4	0.3	0.3	0.3
Manufacturing	33.5	33.1	33.2	33.0	32.5	40.5	36.4	35.9	35.3	34.3
Non-tradeables										
Electricity	3.7	3.7	3.5	3.6	3.6	1.7	1.7	1.7	1.6	1.6
Construction	10.0	8.0	7.9	8.0	8.3	11.2	9.9	10.0	10.2	10.4
Wholesale and retail trade, restaurants and hotels	19.5	19.9	20.3	20.2	20.2	21.4	23.9	24.2	24.5	24.8
Transport, storage and communication	6.8	7.5	7.5	7.8	8.0	9.6	10.2	10.2	10.2	10.3
Finance, insurance, real estate and business services	17.5	18.8	18.6	18.8	19.0	8.4	9.9	10.1	10.3	10.5
Community, social and personal services	4.2	4.7	4.7	4.8	4.7	5.1	6.3	6.3	6.4	6.6

B. Industrial sector performance

	Productivity growth (sector GDP/sector employment)					Investment share, current prices (per cent of total)				
	1980	1989	1990	1991	1992	1980	1989	1990	1991	1992
Tradeables										
Agriculture	8.7	0.7	4.2	-6.5	-3.5	6.4	4.5	4.8	4.6	4.1
Mining and quarrying	2.5	-2.5	8.8	-5.1	6.5	0.4	0.3	0.2	..	..
Manufacturing	2.1	3.5	4.1	2.3	2.5	20.5	18.1	19.4	..	..
Non-tradeables										
Electricity	5.9	10.4	2.2	4.0	3.9	6.9	5.1	4.9	..	..
Construction	0.0	2.5	-0.4	0.7	2.4	2.8	2.3	2.2	..	..
Wholesale and retail trade, restaurants and hotels	0.0	0.8	3.0	-0.5	-0.1	..	..	..	..	..
Transport, storage and communication	4.8	5.0	3.6	4.4	2.7	..	..	..	..	..
Finance, insurance, real estate and business services	3.2	1.2	-0.5	0.1	0.1	..	..	..	..	..
Community, social and personal services	1.4	1.9	3.2	0.2	-1.7	..	..	..	..	..

148

Table K. **Production structure and performance indicators** *(cont'd)*

	Numbers of entreprises (per cent of total)					Numbers of employees (per cent of total)				
	1971	1980	1989	1990	1991	1971	1980	1989	1990	1991
C. Other indicators										
Enterprises ranged by size of employees										
1 to 4	..	18.3	40.4	38.4	37.7		0.3	0.7	0.7	0.7
5 to 49	57.9	49.0	37.7	38.6	38.8	11.19	11.2	12.4	12.2	12.4
50 to 499	38.3	29.6	20.0	20.9	21.5	48.6	46.6	48.9	49.8	51.6
more than 500	3.9	3.1	2.0	2.1	2.0	40.2	41.9	38.0	37.3	35.4
	1983	1984	1985	1986	1987	1988	1989	1990	1991	1992
R&D as percentage of manufacturing output	4.37	4.65	4.74	5.13	5.40	5.42	5.65	6.00	6.62	7.11

Source: OECD, *National accounts*; Österreichisches Statistisches Handbuch.

BASIC STATISTICS

BASIC STATISTICS:

INTERNATIONAL COMPARISONS

	Units	Reference period [1]	Australia	Austria
Population				
Total	Thousands	1992	17 489	7 884
Inhabitants per sq. km	Number	1992	2	94
Net average annual increase over previous 10 years	%	1992	1.4	0.4
Employment				
Civilian employment (CE)[2]	Thousands	1992	7 637	3 546
Of which: Agriculture	% of CE		5.3	7.1
Industry	% of CE		23.8	35.6
Services	% of CE		71	57.4
Gross domestic product (GDP)				
At current prices and current exchange rates	Bill. US$	1992	296.6	186.2
Per capita	US$		16 959	23 616
At current prices using current PPPs[3]	Bill. US$	1992	294.5	142
Per capita	US$		16 800	18 017
Average annual volume growth over previous 5 years	%	1992	2	3.4
Gross fixed capital formation (GFCF)	% of GDP	1992	19.7	25
Of which: Machinery and equipment	% of GDP		9.3	9.9
Residential construction	% of GDP		5.1	5.7
Average annual volume growth over previous 5 years	%	1992	–1	5.1
Gross saving ratio[4]	% of GDP	1992	15.6	25.1
General government				
Current expenditure on goods and services	% of GDP	1992	18.5	18.4
Current disbursements[5]	% of GDP	1992	36.9	46.2
Current receipts	% of GDP	1992	33.1	48.3
Net official development assistance	% of GNP	1992	0.33	0.3
Indicators of living standards				
Private consumption per capita using current PPPs[3]	US$	1992	10 527	9 951
Passenger cars, per 1 000 inhabitants	Number	1990	430	382
Telephones, per 1 000 inhabitants	Number	1990	448	589
Television sets, per 1 000 inhabitants	Number	1989	484	475
Doctors, per 1 000 inhabitants	Number	1991	2	2.1
Infant mortality per 1 000 live births	Number	1991	7.1	7.4
Wages and prices (average annual increase over previous 5 years)				
Wages (earnings or rates according to availability)	%	1992	5	5.4
Consumer prices	%	1992	5.2	3
Foreign trade				
Exports of goods, fob*	Mill. US$	1992	42 844	44 361
As % of GDP	%		14.4	23.8
Average annual increase over previous 5 years	%		10.1	10.4
Imports of goods, cif*	Mill. US$	1992	40 751	54 038
As % of GDP	%		13.7	29
Average annual increase over previous 5 years	%		8.6	10.7
Total official reserves[6]	Mill. SDRs	1992	8 152	9 006
As ratio of average monthly imports of goods	Ratio		2.4	2

* At current prices and exchange rates.
1. Unless otherwise stated.
2. According to the definitions used in OECD *Labour Force Statistics*.
3. PPPs = Purchasing Power Parities.
4. Gross saving = Gross national disposable income minus private and government consumption.
5. Current disbursements = Current expenditure on goods and services plus current transfers and payments of property income.
6. Gold included in reserves is valued at 35 SDRs per ounce. End of year.
7. Including Luxembourg.

EMPLOYMENT OPPORTUNITIES

Economics Department, OECD

The Economics Department of the OECD offers challenging and rewarding opportunities to economists interested in applied policy analysis in an international environment. The Department's concerns extend across the entire field of economic policy analysis, both macroeconomic and microeconomic. Its main task is to provide, for discussion by committees of senior officials from Member countries, documents and papers dealing with current policy concerns. Within this programme of work, three major responsibilities are:

- to prepare regular surveys of the economies of individual Member countries;
- to issue full twice-yearly reviews of the economic situation and prospects of the OECD countries in the context of world economic trends;
- to analyse specific policy issues in a medium-term context for the OECD as a whole, and to a lesser extent for the non-OECD countries.

The documents prepared for these purposes, together with much of the Department's other economic work, appear in published form in the *OECD Economic Outlook, OECD Economic Surveys, OECD Economic Studies* and the Department's *Working Papers* series.

The Department maintains a world econometric model, INTERLINK, which plays an important role in the preparation of the policy analyses and twice-yearly projections. The availability of extensive cross-country data bases and good computer resources facilitates comparative empirical analysis, much of which is incorporated into the model.

The Department is made up of about 80 professional economists from a variety of backgrounds and Member countries. Most projects are carried out by small teams and last from four to eighteen months. Within the Department, ideas and points of view are widely discussed; there is a lively professional interchange, and all professional staff have the opportunity to contribute actively to the programme of work.

Skills the Economics Department is looking for:

a) Solid competence in using the tools of both microeconomic and macroeconomic theory to answer policy questions. Experience indicates that this normally requires the equivalent of a Ph.D. in economics or substantial relevant professional experience to compensate for a lower degree.

b) Solid knowledge of economic statistics and quantitative methods; this includes how to identify data, estimate structural relationships, apply basic techniques of time series analysis, and test hypotheses. It is essential to be able to interpret results sensibly in an economic policy context.

c) A keen interest in and extensive knowledge of policy issues, economic developments and their political/social contexts.

d) Interest and experience in analysing questions posed by policy-makers and presenting the results to them effectively and judiciously. Thus, work experience in government agencies or policy research institutions is an advantage.

e) The ability to write clearly, effectively, and to the point. The OECD is a bilingual organisation with French and English as the official languages. Candidates must have excellent knowledge of one of these languages, and some knowledge of the other. Knowledge of other languages might also be an advantage for certain posts.

f) For some posts, expertise in a particular area may be important, but a successful candidate is expected to be able to work on a broader range of topics relevant to the work of the Department. Thus, except in rare cases, the Department does not recruit narrow specialists.

g) The Department works on a tight time schedule with strict deadlines. Moreover, much of the work in the Department is carried out in small groups. Thus, the ability to work with other economists from a variety of cultural and professional backgrounds, to supervise junior staff, and to produce work on time is important.

General information

The salary for recruits depends on educational and professional background. Positions carry a basic salary from FF 305 700 or FF 377 208 for Administrators (economists) and from FF 438 348 for Principal Administrators (senior economists). This may be supplemented by expatriation and/or family allowances, depending on nationality, residence and family situation. Initial appointments are for a fixed term of two to three years.

Vacancies are open to candidates from OECD Member countries. The Organisation seeks to maintain an appropriate balance between female and male staff and among nationals from Member countries.

For further information on employment opportunities in the Economics Department, contact:

Administrative Unit
Economics Department
OECD
2, rue André-Pascal
75775 PARIS CEDEX 16
FRANCE

E-Mail: compte.esadmin@oecd.org

Applications citing ''ECSUR'', together with a detailed *curriculum vitae* in English or French, should be sent to the Head of Personnel at the above address.

MAIN SALES OUTLETS OF OECD PUBLICATIONS
PRINCIPAUX POINTS DE VENTE DES PUBLICATIONS DE L'OCDE

ARGENTINA – ARGENTINE
Carlos Hirsch S.R.L.
Galería Güemes, Florida 165, 4° Piso
1333 Buenos Aires Tel. (1) 331.1787 y 331.2391
Telefax: (1) 331.1787

AUSTRALIA – AUSTRALIE
D.A. Information Services
648 Whitehorse Road, P.O.B 163
Mitcham, Victoria 3132 Tel. (03) 873.4411
Telefax: (03) 873.5679

AUSTRIA – AUTRICHE
Gerold & Co.
Graben 31
Wien I Tel. (0222) 533.50.14

BELGIUM – BELGIQUE
Jean De Lannoy
Avenue du Roi 202
B-1060 Bruxelles Tel. (02) 538.51.69/538.08.41
Telefax: (02) 538.08.41

CANADA
Renouf Publishing Company Ltd.
1294 Algoma Road
Ottawa, ON K1B 3W8 Tel. (613) 741.4333
Telefax: (613) 741.5439
Stores:
61 Sparks Street
Ottawa, ON K1P 5R1 Tel. (613) 238.8985
211 Yonge Street
Toronto, ON M5B 1M4 Tel. (416) 363.3171
Telefax: (416)363.59.63
Les Éditions La Liberté Inc.
3020 Chemin Sainte-Foy
Sainte-Foy, PQ G1X 3V6 Tel. (418) 658.3763
Telefax: (418) 658.3763

Federal Publications Inc.
165 University Avenue, Suite 701
Toronto, ON M5H 3B8 Tel. (416) 860.1611
Telefax: (416) 860.1608
Les Publications Fédérales
1185 Université
Montréal, QC H3B 3A7 Tel. (514) 954.1633
Telefax : (514) 954.1635

CHINA – CHINE
China National Publications Import
Export Corporation (CNPIEC)
16 Gongti E. Road, Chaoyang District
P.O. Box 88 or 50
Beijing 100704 PR Tel. (01) 506.6688
Telefax: (01) 506.3101

CZECH REPUBLIC – RÉPUBLIQUE TCHÈQUE
Artia Pegas Press Ltd.
Narodni Trida 25
POB 825
111 21 Praha 1 Tel. 26.65.68
Telefax: 26.20.81

DENMARK – DANEMARK
Munksgaard Book and Subscription Service
35, Nørre Søgade, P.O. Box 2148
DK-1016 København K Tel. (33) 12.85.70
Telefax: (33) 12.93.87

EGYPT – ÉGYPTE
Middle East Observer
41 Sherif Street
Cairo Tel. 392.6919
Telefax: 360-6804

FINLAND – FINLANDE
Akateeminen Kirjakauppa
Keskuskatu 1, P.O. Box 128
00100 Helsinki
Subscription Services/Agence d'abonnements :
P.O. Box 23
00371 Helsinki Tel. (358 0) 12141
Telefax: (358 0) 121.4450

FRANCE
OECD/OCDE
Mail Orders/Commandes par correspondance:
2, rue André-Pascal
75775 Paris Cedex 16 Tel. (33-1) 45.24.82.00
Telefax: (33-1) 49.10.42.76
Telex: 640048 OCDE
Orders via Minitel, France only/
Commandes par Minitel, France exclusivement :
36 15 OCDE

OECD Bookshop/Librairie de l'OCDE :
33, rue Octave-Feuillet
75016 Paris Tel. (33-1) 45.24.81.67
(33-1) 45.24.81.81

Documentation Française
29, quai Voltaire
75007 Paris Tel. 40.15.70.00

Gibert Jeune (Droit-Économie)
6, place Saint-Michel
75006 Paris Tel. 43.25.91.19

Librairie du Commerce International
10, avenue d'Iéna
75016 Paris Tel. 40.73.34.60

Librairie Dunod
Université Paris-Dauphine
Place du Maréchal de Lattre de Tassigny
75016 Paris Tel. (1) 44.05.40.13

Librairie Lavoisier
11, rue Lavoisier
75008 Paris Tel. 42.65.39.95

Librairie L.G.D.J. - Montchrestien
20, rue Soufflot
75005 Paris Tel. 46.33.89.85

Librairie des Sciences Politiques
30, rue Saint-Guillaume
75007 Paris Tel. 45.48.36.02

P.U.F.
49, boulevard Saint-Michel
75005 Paris Tel. 43.25.83.40

Librairie de l'Université
12a, rue Nazareth
13100 Aix-en-Provence Tel. (16) 42.26.18.08

Documentation Française
165, rue Garibaldi
69003 Lyon Tel. (16) 78.63.32.23

Librairie Decitre
29, place Bellecour
69002 Lyon Tel. (16) 72.40.54.54

GERMANY – ALLEMAGNE
OECD Publications and Information Centre
August-Bebel-Allee 6
D-53175 Bonn Tel. (0228) 959.120
Telefax: (0228) 959.12.17

GREECE – GRÈCE
Librairie Kauffmann
Mavrokordatou 9
106 78 Athens Tel. (01) 32.55.321
Telefax: (01) 36.33.967

HONG-KONG
Swindon Book Co. Ltd.
13–15 Lock Road
Kowloon, Hong Kong Tel. 2376.2062
Telefax: 2376.0685

HUNGARY – HONGRIE
Euro Info Service
Margitsziget, Európa Ház
1138 Budapest Tel. (1) 111.62.16
Telefax : (1) 111.60.61

ICELAND – ISLANDE
Mál Mog Menning
Laugavegi 18, Pósthólf 392
121 Reykjavik Tel. 162.35.23

INDIA – INDE
Oxford Book and Stationery Co.
Scindia House
New Delhi 110001 Tel.(11) 331.5896/5308
Telefax: (11) 332.5993
17 Park Street
Calcutta 700016 Tel. 240832

INDONESIA – INDONÉSIE
Pdii-Lipi
P.O. Box 4298
Jakarta 12042 Tel. (21) 573.34.67
Telefax: (21) 573.34.67

IRELAND – IRLANDE
Government Supplies Agency
Publications Section
4/5 Harcourt Road
Dublin 2 Tel. 661.31.11
Telefax: 478.06.45

ISRAEL
Praedicta
5 Shatner Street
P.O. Box 34030
Jerusalem 91430 Tel. (2) 52.84.90/1/2
Telefax: (2) 52.84.93

R.O.Y.
P.O. Box 13056
Tel Aviv 61130 Tél. (3) 49.61.08
Telefax (3) 544.60.39

ITALY – ITALIE
Libreria Commissionaria Sansoni
Via Duca di Calabria 1/1
50125 Firenze Tel. (055) 64.54.15
Telefax: (055) 64.12.57
Via Bartolini 29
20155 Milano Tel. (02) 36.50.83

Editrice e Libreria Herder
Piazza Montecitorio 120
00186 Roma Tel. 679.46.28
Telefax: 678.47.51

Libreria Hoepli
Via Hoepli 5
20121 Milano Tel. (02) 86.54.46
Telefax: (02) 805.28.86

Libreria Scientifica
Dott. Lucio de Biasio 'Aeiou'
Via Coronelli, 6
20146 Milano Tel. (02) 48.95.45.52
Telefax: (02) 48.95.45.48

JAPAN – JAPON
OECD Publications and Information Centre
Landic Akasaka Building
2-3-4 Akasaka, Minato-ku
Tokyo 107 Tel. (81.3) 3586.2016
Telefax: (81.3) 3584.7929

KOREA – CORÉE
Kyobo Book Centre Co. Ltd.
P.O. Box 1658, Kwang Hwa Moon
Seoul Tel. 730.78.91
Telefax: 735.00.30

MALAYSIA – MALAISIE
University of Malaya Bookshop
University of Malaya
P.O. Box 1127, Jalan Pantai Baru
59700 Kuala Lumpur
Malaysia Tel. 756.5000/756.5425
Telefax: 756.3246

MEXICO – MEXIQUE
Revistas y Periodicos Internacionales S.A. de C.V.
Florencia 57 - 1004
Mexico, D.F. 06600 Tel. 207.81.00
Telefax : 208.39.79

NETHERLANDS – PAYS-BAS
SDU Uitgeverij Plantijnstraat
Externe Fondsen
Postbus 20014
2500 EA's-Gravenhage   Tel. (070) 37.89.880
Voor bestellingen: Telefax: (070) 34.75.778

**NEW ZEALAND
NOUVELLE-ZÉLANDE**
Legislation Services
P.O. Box 12418
Thorndon, Wellington   Tel. (04) 496.5652
          Telefax: (04) 496.5698

NORWAY – NORVÈGE
Narvesen Info Center – NIC
Bertrand Narvesens vei 2
P.O. Box 6125 Etterstad
0602 Oslo 6   Tel. (022) 57.33.00
          Telefax: (022) 68.19.01

PAKISTAN
Mirza Book Agency
65 Shahrah Quaid-E-Azam
Lahore 54000   Tel. (42) 353.601
          Telefax: (42) 231.730

PHILIPPINE – PHILIPPINES
International Book Center
5th Floor, Filipinas Life Bldg.
Ayala Avenue
Metro Manila   Tel. 81.96.76
          Telex 23312 RHP PH

PORTUGAL
Livraria Portugal
Rua do Carmo 70-74
Apart. 2681
1200 Lisboa   Tel.: (01) 347.49.82/5
          Telefax: (01) 347.02.64

SINGAPORE – SINGAPOUR
Gower Asia Pacific Pte Ltd.
Golden Wheel Building
41, Kallang Pudding Road, No. 04-03
Singapore 1334   Tel. 741.5166
          Telefax: 742.9356

SPAIN – ESPAGNE
Mundi-Prensa Libros S.A.
Castelló 37, Apartado 1223
Madrid 28001   Tel. (91) 431.33.99
          Telefax: (91) 575.39.98

Libreria Internacional AEDOS
Consejo de Ciento 391
08009 – Barcelona   Tel. (93) 488.30.09
          Telefax: (93) 487.76.59
Llibreria de la Generalitat
Palau Moja
Rambla dels Estudis, 118
08002 – Barcelona
          (Subscripcions) Tel. (93) 318.80.12
          (Publicacions) Tel. (93) 302.67.23
          Telefax: (93) 412.18.54

SRI LANKA
Centre for Policy Research
c/o Colombo Agencies Ltd.
No. 300-304, Galle Road
Colombo 3   Tel. (1) 574240, 573551-2
          Telefax: (1) 575394, 510711

SWEDEN – SUÈDE
Fritzes Information Center
Box 16356
Regeringsgatan 12
106 47 Stockholm   Tel. (08) 690.90.90
          Telefax: (08) 20.50.21
Subscription Agency/Agence d'abonnements :
Wennergren-Williams Info AB
P.O. Box 1305
171 25 Solna   Tel. (08) 705.97.50
          Téléfax : (08) 27.00.71

SWITZERLAND – SUISSE
Maditec S.A. (Books and Periodicals - Livres
et périodiques)
Chemin des Palettes 4
Case postale 266
1020 Renens VD 1   Tel. (021) 635.08.65
          Telefax: (021) 635.07.80

Librairie Payot S.A.
4, place Pépinet
CP 3212
1002 Lausanne   Tel. (021) 341.33.47
          Telefax: (021) 341.33.45

Librairie Unilivres
6, rue de Candolle
1205 Genève   Tel. (022) 320.26.23
          Telefax: (022) 329.73.18

Subscription Agency/Agence d'abonnements :
Dynapresse Marketing S.A.
38 avenue Vibert
1227 Carouge   Tel.: (022) 308.07.89
          Telefax : (022) 308.07.99

See also – Voir aussi :
OECD Publications and Information Centre
August-Bebel-Allee 6
D-53175 Bonn (Germany)   Tel. (0228) 959.120
          Telefax: (0228) 959.12.17

TAIWAN – FORMOSE
Good Faith Worldwide Int'l. Co. Ltd.
9th Floor, No. 118, Sec. 2
Chung Hsiao E. Road
Taipei   Tel. (02) 391.7396/391.7397
          Telefax: (02) 394.9176

THAILAND – THAÏLANDE
Suksit Siam Co. Ltd.
113, 115 Fuang Nakhon Rd.
Opp. Wat Rajbopith
Bangkok 10200   Tel. (662) 225.9531/2
          Telefax: (662) 222.5188

TURKEY – TURQUIE
Kültür Yayinlari Is-Türk Ltd. Sti.
Atatürk Bulvari No. 191/Kat 13
Kavaklidere/Ankara   Tel. 428.11.40 Ext. 2458
Dolmabahce Cad. No. 29
Besiktas/Istanbul   Tel. 260.71.88
          Telex: 43482B

UNITED KINGDOM – ROYAUME-UNI
HMSO
Gen. enquiries   Tel. (071) 873 0011
Postal orders only:
P.O. Box 276, London SW8 5DT
Personal Callers HMSO Bookshop
49 High Holborn, London WC1V 6HB
          Telefax: (071) 873 8200
Branches at: Belfast, Birmingham, Bristol, Edin-
burgh, Manchester

UNITED STATES – ÉTATS-UNIS
OECD Publications and Information Centre
2001 L Street N.W., Suite 700
Washington, D.C. 20036-4910 Tel. (202) 785.6323
          Telefax: (202) 785.0350

VENEZUELA
Libreria del Este
Avda F. Miranda 52, Aptdo. 60337
Edificio Galipán
Caracas 106   Tel. 951.1705/951.2307/951.1297
          Telegram: Libreste Caracas

Subscription to OECD periodicals may also be
placed through main subscription agencies.

Les abonnements aux publications périodiques de
l'OCDE peuvent être souscrits auprès des
principales agences d'abonnement.

Orders and inquiries from countries where Distribu-
tors have not yet been appointed should be sent to:
OECD Publications Service, 2 rue André-Pascal,
75775 Paris Cedex 16, France.

Les commandes provenant de pays où l'OCDE n'a
pas encore désigné de distributeur peuvent être
adressées à : OCDE, Service des Publications,
2, rue André-Pascal, 75775 Paris Cedex 16, France.

1-1995